COLOSSIANS-PHILEMON: A BEGINNING-INTERMEDIATE GREEK READER

COLOSSIANS-PHILEMON
A BEGINNING-INTERMEDIATE GREEK READER

ROY R. JEAL

GH
GLOSSAHOUSE
WILMORE, KY
www.glossahouse.com

Colossians-Philemon: A Beginning-Intermediate Greek Reader

© 2015 by GlossaHouse

All rights reserved. No part of this work may be reproduced or transmitted in any form or by any means, electronic or mechanical, including photocopying and recording, or by means of any information storage or retrieval system, except as may be expressly permitted by the 1976 Copyright Act or in writing from the publisher. Requests for permission should be addressed in writing to:

GlossaHouse, LLC
110 Callis Circle
Wilmore, KY 40390

Publisher's Cataloging-in-Publication Data
Jeal, Roy R.,
 Colossians-Philemon: A Beginning-Intermediate Greek Reader/ Roy R. Jeal
  p. cm. — (AGROS Series)
Includes Appendices.
ISBN-13: 978-1942697015
ISBN-10: 1942697015
1. Religion: Biblical Reference - Language Study. 2. Religion: Biblical Studies - New Testament. 3. Religion: Biblical Studies – Paul's Letters. I. Title. II. Series (AGROS)
Library of Congress Control Number: 2015933966

SBLGNT is the *The Greek New Testament: SBL Edition*. Copyright 2010 Society of Biblical Literature and Logos Bible Software [ISBN 978-1-58983-535-1]. The SBLGNT text can be found online at http://sblgnt.com. Information about the "Society of Biblical Literature" can be found at http://sbl-site.org and "Logos Bible Software" at http://logos.com.

The fonts used to create this work are available from www.linguistsoftware.com/lgku.htm.

Babel Lexicography (BabLex), licensed by J. Klay Harrison and Chad M. Foster, 2012.

Koine Greek Paradigm Chart by J. Klay Harrison in consultation with Fredrick J. Long.

Cover Design by T. Michael W. Halcomb.
Book Design by Fredrick J. Long

This Series is dedicated to all who have struggled to make Greek a regular part of their study of Scripture.

Contents

AGROS Series Introduction	ix
List of Abbreviations	x
Preface to the Beginning-Intermediate Greek Readers	1
How to Use the Beginning-Intermediate Greek Readers	2
Introduction to the SBLGNT	7
ΠΡΟΣ ΚΟΛΟΣΣΑΕΙΣ	23
ΠΡΟΣ ΦΙΛΗΜΟΝΑ	63
APPENDICES	73

APPENDIX I
    SBLGNT Apparatus   75
    Differences between the SBLGNT and NA28   78
APPENDIX II
    Vocabulary 50 Times or More Sorted by Frequency   81
APPENDIX III
    Vocabulary 50 Times or More Sorted Alphabetically   91
APPENDIX IV
    Koine Greek Paradigm Charts   103

AGROS
ACCESSIBLE GREEK RESOURCES AND ONLINE STUDIES

SERIES EDITORS
T. Michael W. Halcomb
Fredrick J. Long

AGROS EDITORIAL BOARD
Chad M. Foster
T. Michael W. Halcomb
Fredrick J. Long

BEGINNING-INTERMEDIATE GREEK READER EDITOR
Fredrick J. Long

VOLUME EDITORS
Jordan L. Day
Fredrick J. Long

GlossaHouse
Wilmore, KY

AGROS

The Greek term ἀγρός is a field where seeds are planted and growth occurs. It also can denote a small village or community that forms around such a field. The type of community envisioned here is one that attends to Holy Scripture, particularly one that encourages the use of biblical Greek. Accessible Greek Resources and Online Studies (AGROS) is a tiered curriculum suite featuring innovative readers, grammars, specialized studies, and other exegetical resources to encourage and foster the exegetical use of biblical Greek. The goal of AGROS is to facilitate the creation and publication of innovative and inexpensive print and digital resources for the exposition of Scripture within the context of the global church. The AGROS curriculum includes five tiers, and each tier is indicated on the book's cover: Tier 1 (Beginning I), Tier 2 (Beginning II), Tier 3 (Intermediate I), Tier 4 (Intermediate II), and Tier 5 (Advanced). There are also two resource tracks: Conversational and Translational. Both involve intensive study of morphology, grammar, syntax, and discourse features. The conversational track specifically values the spoken word, and the enhanced learning associated with speaking a language in actual conversation. The translational track values the written word, and encourages analytical study to aide in understanding and translating biblical Greek and other Greek literature. The two resource tracks complement one another and can be pursued independently or together.

AGROS EDITORIAL BOARD
Chad M. Foster
T. Michael W. Halcomb
Fredrick J. Long

ABBREVIATIONS

1st	first person
2nd	second person
3rd	third person
F, ϝ	*vau* or digamma (an old Greek letter)
abl.	ablative
abs.	absolute, absolutely
acc.	accusative
act.	active
add.	additional, additionally
adj.	adjective
adv.	adverb, adverbial, adverbially
alt.	alternately
ans.	answer
ante.	antecedent
aor.	aorist
app.	apposition, appositional
art.	article
attrib.	attributive, attributively
aug.	augment
Barclay	Newman, Barclay M., ed. *A Concise Greek-English Dictionary of the New Testament.* Stuttgart: Deutsche Bibelgesellschaft, 1993.
BDAG	Bauer, F., F. W. Danker, et al., eds. *A Greek-English Lexicon of the New Testament and Other Early Christian Literature.* 3rd ed. Chicago: University of Chicago Press, 2000.
beg.	beginning
btw.	between

cmpd.	compound
comp.	comparative, comparatively
conj.	conjunction
constr.	construct, construction.
correl.	correlative
corresp.	corresponding, correspondingly
dat.	dative
dem.	demonstrative
dep.	deponent
diph.	diphtong
dir.	direct
dissim.	dissimilate, dissimilation
ditrans.	ditransitive (trivalent)
ECM	Aland, Barbara, Kurt Aland, Gerd Mink and Klaus Wachtel, eds. *Novum Testamentum Graecum: Editio Critica Maior*, vol. 4: *Catholic Letters*. 4 installments. Stuttgart: Deutsche Biblegesellschaft, 1997–2005.
e.g.	exempli gratia, Latin: "for example"
em.	emendation
emph.	emphatic
encl.	enclitic
equiv.	equivalent
euphem.	euphemism
fem.	feminine
fig.	figurative, figuratively
fut.	future
gen.	genitive, genitival
GNT	Greek New Testament

Greeven	Huck, Albert. *Synopse der drei ersten Evangelien/ Synopsis of the First Three Gospels*. 13th ed. Revised by Heinrich Greeven. Tübingen: Mohr Siebeck, 1981.
hist.	historical
Holmes	Michael W. Holmes
imper.	impersonal (avalent)
impf.	imperfect
impv.	imperative
indef.	indefinite
indic.	indicative
indir.	indirect
inf.	infinitive
init.	initial
instr.	instrumental
inter.	interrogative
intrans.	intransitive (monovalent)
irreg.	irregular
L&N	Louw, Johannes P., and Eugene A. Nida, eds. *Greek-English Lexicon of the New Testament: Based on Semantic Domains*. 2 vols. 2nd ed. New York: United Bible Societies, 1989.
length.	lengthen, lengthened
lit.	literally
loc.	locative
LSJ	Liddell, Henry G., R. Scott, H. S. Jones, and R. McKenzie, eds. *A Greek-English Lexicon*. Rev. 9th ed. Oxford: Clarendon, 1996.

masc.	masculine
mid.	middle
metaph.	metaphor, metaphorical
MH	morphology help
Mounce	Mounce, William D. *The Morphology of Biblical Greek*. Grand Rapids: Zondervan, 1994.
Muraoka	Muraoka, T. *A Greek-English Lexicon of the Septuagint*. Louvain: Peeters, 2009.
neg.	negative, negate(d)
neut.	neuter
nom.	nominative, nominal
NA	Greek text of the NA^{27} and UBS^4
NA^{27}	Aland, Barbara, K. Aland, J. Karavidopoulos, C. M. Martini, and B. M. Metzger, eds. *Novum Testamentum Graece*. 27th ed. Stuttgart: Deutsche Bibelgesellschaft, 1993.
NA^{28}	Aland, Barbara, K. Aland, J. Karavidopoulos, C. M. Martini, B. M. Metzger, and Institute for New Testament Textual Research, eds. *Novum Testamentum Graece*, 28th ed. Stuttgart: Deutsche Bibelgesellschaft, 2012.
NIV	Goodrich, Richard J., and Albert L. Lukaszewski, eds., *A Reader's Greek New Testament*. Grand Rapids: Zondervan, 2003.
NRSV	New Revised Standard Version
occ.	occur, occurrence
obj.	object
opt.	optative
paren.	parenthetical
pass.	passive
per.	person, personal

periphr.	periphrastic
pf.	perfect, perfective
pl.	plural
plpf.	pluperfect
pos.	positive
poss.	possessive
post.	postcedent
prec.	preceding
pred.	predicate
pref.	prefix, prefixed
prep.	preposition, prepositional
pres.	present
pron.	pronoun
prtc.	participle
reduc.	reduction
redupl.	reduplicate, reduplication
ref.	reference
reflex.	reflexive
rel.	relative
RP	Robinson, Maurice A., and William G. Pierpont, eds. *The New Testament in the Original Greek: Byzantine Textform 2005.* Southborough, Mass.: Chilton, 2005.
SBL	Society of Biblical Literature
SBLGNT	Holmes, Michael W. *The Greek New Testament: SBL Edition.* Atlanta: Society of Biblical Literature, 2010. http://sblgnt.com/.
SBLGNT[app]	Apparatus of SBLGNT
sg.	singular
Smyth	Smyth, Herbert Weir. *Greek Grammar.* Revised by Gordon M. Messing. Harvard Press, 1984.

subj.	subjunctive
subst.	substantival, substantive
suf.	suffix, suffixed
superl.	superlative
suppl.	suppletive
syn.	synonym
TDNT	Friedrich, Gerhard, and Gerhard Kittel, eds. *Theological Dictionary of the New Testament*. 10 vols., tr. by G. W. Bromiley. Grand Rapids, Mich.: Eerdmans, 1964–76.
TH	Translation Help
TLNT	Spicq, Ceslas. *Theological Lexicon of the New Testament*. 3 vols. Peabody, Mass: Hendrickson, 1994.
TR	Textus Receptus ("Received Text")
trans.	transitive (divalent)
translit.	transliteration (of a loan word into Greek)
Treg	Tregelles, Samuel Prideaux. *The Greek New Testament, Edited from Ancient Authorities, with their Various Readings in Full, and the Latin Version of Jerome*. London: Bagster; Stewart, 1857–1879.
Treg^{marg}	margin of Treg
Trenchard	Trenchard, Warren C. *Complete Vocabulary Guide to the Greek New Testament*. Rev. ed. Grand Rapids, Mich.: Zondervan, 1998.
UBS^4	Aland, B., K. Aland, J. Karavidopoulos, C. M. Martini, and B. M. Metzger, eds. *The Greek New Testament*. 4th rev. ed. New York: United Bible Societies, 2006.
voc.	vocative

WH	Hort, Fenton John Anthony, and Brooke Foss Westcott. *The New Testament in the Original Greek*. 2 vols. Cambridge: Macmillan, 1881.
WH[app]	*Appendix* (vol. 2 of WH)
WH[marg]	margin of WH
Works (TJ)	Jackson, Thomas, ed. *The Works of the Rev. John Wesley, M.A.* 14 vols. Grand Rapids: Baker, 1978.

PREFACE TO THE BEGINNING-INTERMEDIATE GREEK READERS

And men who speak the Latin tongue, of whom are those I have undertaken to instruct, need two other languages for the knowledge of Scripture, Hebrew and Greek, that they may have recourse to the original texts if the endless diversity of the Latin translators throw them into doubt.
— Saint Augustine, *De Doctrina Christiana* 2.11.16

Do I understand Greek and Hebrew? Otherwise, how can I undertake, (as every Minister does,) not only to explain books which are written therein, but to defend them against all opponents? Am I not at the mercy of everyone who does understand, or even pretends to understand, the original? For which way can I confute his pretense? Do I understand the language of the Old Testament? critically? at all? Can I read into English one of David's Psalms, or even the first chapter of Genesis? Do I understand the language of the New Testament? Am I a critical master of it? Have I enough of it even to read into English the first chapter of St. Luke? If not, how many years did I spend at school? How many at the University? And what was I doing all those years? Ought not shame to cover my face?

— John Wesley, "An Address to the Clergy," *Works* (TJ) X:491.

These authorities are aptly quoted by J. Klay Harrison in the preface to the *1-3 John: A General Reader*. Hebrew and Greek are foundational languages for the study of Scripture. For beginning students, the next steps after initially learning the languages are big ones. The goal for the *Beginning-Intermediate Greek Readers* within the AGROS series is to encourage both the retention of and the progress in Greek through reading the Greek NT itself. These *Beginning-Intermediate Greek Readers* provide vocabulary, translational, and morphological helps, assuming that beginning Greek students have acquired beginning grammar and vocabulary occurring 50 times or more. So, these readers provide meanings for words occurring less than 50 times in the Greek NT, offer translation helps for more difficult grammatical constructions, and give morphological explanations for challenging formations of Greek words.

Fredrick J. Long
Series Editor of AGROS Beginning-Intermediate Greek Readers

How to Use the Beginning-Intermediate Greek Readers

The Beginning-Intermediate Greek Readers are designed to be a user-friendly guide for reading the GNT. They will provide footnotes with all vocabulary that occurs 49 times or less, morphological and textual helps, and variants between the SBLGNT and the standard critical editions of the GNT. Additionally, each chapter is introduced with a vocabulary list of infrequent words that occur within the chapter. The list is sorted by word frequency as found in the chapter, arranged from most to least frequent.

The Greek Text

The main Greek text used here is *The Greek New Testament: SBL Edition* (SBLGNT). This edition is a critical text of the GNT and includes a text-critical apparatus. The SBLGNT text and apparatus are explained in the "Introduction to the SBLGNT," which follows this section. The "Introduction to the SBLGNT" expounds not only how the SBLGNT text was assembled but also how to use the text-critical apparatus found in Appendix I. The introduction was written by Michael Holmes and is also found in *The Greek New Testament: SBL Edition*.

> SBLGNT is the *The Greek New Testament: SBL Edition*. Copyright 2010 Society of Biblical Literature and Logos Bible Software [ISBN 978-1-58983-535-1]. The SBLGNT text can be found online at http://sblgnt.com. Information about the "Society of Biblical Literature" can be found at http://sbl-site.org and "Logos Bible Software" at http://logos.com.

The Text-Critical Apparatus

The text-critical markings found in the SBLGNT point the reader to the apparatus, which is included in Appendix I. For an explanation of the text critical marks and the apparatus, please see "Introduction to the SBLGNT."

How to Use the Beginning-Intermediate Greek Readers

The Footnotes

For ease of reading, this book uses footnotes as a guide through the GNT. The footnotes provide four categories of information; 1) lexical aid, 2) morphology help (MH), 3) translation help (TH), and 4) NA (NA$^{27\text{-}28}$ and UBS^4) variants. Each category is described below.

1) If a Greek word occurs 49 times or less in the GNT, then lexical aid is provided in a footnote. First, the Greek word is provided in lexical (dictionary) form. Thus, all verbs are presented in **pres. act. indic. 1st sg.** conjugation. Pronouns and adjectives are shown in **nom. sg. masc.** form followed by the **nom. sg. fem.** and **nom. sg. neut.** endings. The lexical form for a noun is the **nom. sg.** full inflection followed by the **gen. sg.** ending and then the respective article, which indicates gender. After the word's lexical form, glosses are found in italics. These glosses are standard meanings for the Greek word but they are not comprehensive of the word's complete lexical range. Since words only have meaning in context, there are times when a standard gloss is not appropriate for adequate translation. In these instances, a contextual gloss will be suggested in a bold italic font following a semicolon.

e.g., λόγος, ου, ὁ, *word, speech, matter;* ***concept***.

In this example, the Greek word in question is a form of λόγος. Since λόγος is a noun, the fully inflected nom. sg. masc. form (λόγος) is provided. Then follows the gen. ending (ου), which lets the reader know this is a 2nd declension noun. The article (ὁ) is given in nom. sg. masc. inflected form. Since ὁ is masc., the article then indicates λόγος is a masc. noun. Thus, the entire lexical form is λόγος, ου, ὁ. Then, to translate λόγος, the footnote suggests using one of the following standard glosses: *word, speech, matter*. However, it appears these standard glosses do not capture the true meaning of λόγος within the given context. So, the footnote also provides a contextual gloss to better fit this particular context. Thus, here it is suggested that λόγος should be translated as ***concept***.

2) Morphology helps (MH) are also provided in the footnotes. These notes supply difficult parsing, explain word formation, and clarify any morphological issues.

e.g., MH: fut. act. indic. 2ⁿᵈ pl. from μένω = μεν (root) + εσ (tense formative) + ετε (thematic 2ⁿᵈ pl. ending) > μεν + εετε (σ btw. two vowels elides) > μενεῖτε (vowels contract; ε + ε = εῖ).

MH in this footnote denotes the following as morphology help. The particular word in question is μενεῖτε. The parsing is given along with the lexical form. Then a detailed explanation shows step by step how the inflected verb was formed.

3) The third footnote category is the TH, which provides brief explanations for difficult grammar, idioms, morphology, and syntax.

e.g., TH: λόγου is dir.obj. of ἀκούει.

TH in the footnote illustration marks what follows as a translation help. λόγου is the word in question within the main Greek text. The TH is telling the reader that, in this clause, λόγου is functioning as the direct object of the verb ἀκούει.

4) Any difference in spelling between the SBLGNT and the NA are also available in a footnote. This will be evidenced by "NA" has and then the textual difference. Although these variants are presented in the text-critical apparatus found in the Appendix I, they are included in the footnotes for sake of quick reference.

e.g., NA has ῥῆμα.

Here the footnote informs the reader that the NA Greek text has ῥῆμα where the SBLGNT has something different.

THE VOCABULARY AND GLOSSES

The beginning Koinē Greek student should learn every word that occurs in the GNT 50 times or more (310 words). This book includes glosses for these frequent words in the Appendices. They are listed by frequency (for vocabulary retention) and alphabetically (for quick reference). Every word that occurs 49 times or less in the GNT will be glossed in the footnotes. Additionally, each chapter is introduced with a vocabulary list of infrequent words that occur within the chapter. The list is sorted by

How to Use the Beginning-Intermediate Greek Readers

word frequency as found in the chapter, arranged from most to least frequent and then alphabetically.

All glosses are a collaborative effort between the AGORS Editorial Board and Babel Lexicography (BabLex). These glosses are the result of independent research and the consultation of numerous resources, which include but are not limited to: Barclay, BDAG, Muraoka, LSJ, L&N, TDNT, TLNT, and Trenchard. All word frequency is based upon lexical occurrences in the SBLGNT, not the NA.

The goal in establishing vocabulary glosses is to provide accurate yet concise glosses for every word. Knowing that words only have meaning in context, standard glosses will not suffice for every word occurrence. Such is the limit of a gloss. Whenever the standard glosses do not fix the context, a contextual gloss will be available in a footnote.

THE APPENDICES

The appendices include four sections: 1) Apparatus, 2) Vocabulary by Frequency, 3) Vocabulary Alphabetically, and 4) Koinē Greek Paradigm Charts. Each section is described below.

1) **Appendix I: Apparatus.** Throughout the SBLGNT, text-critical marks will point the reader to the SBLGNT Apparatus (SBLGNT[app]) that has been placed in Appendix I. For an explanation of the text-critical marks and the SBLGNT[app], please see the section entitled "Introduction to the SBLGNT." Following the SBLGNT[app], Appendix I also includes a short section explaining any differences between the SBLGNT and ECM (*Novum Testamentum Graecum: Editio Critica Maior*).

2) **Appendix II: Vocabulary by Frequency.** In order to best serve the Koinē Greek student, all vocabulary assumed as known has been sorted from most to least frequent and is included in Appendix II. These 310 words, which occur 50 times or more in the SBLGNT, are available for students wanting to learn or refresh their GNT vocabulary.

3) **Appendix III: Vocabulary Alphabetically.** All vocabulary occurring 50 times or more, which is assumed as known, is sorted alphabetically in Appendix III.

4) **Appendix IV: Koinē Greek Paradigm Charts.** Appendix IV includes the *Koinē Greek Paradigm Charts* by J. Klay Harrison. These charts will be a helpful resource to students having difficulty parsing words or just needing a quick refresher on Greek endings.

INTRODUCTION TO THE SBLGNT[1]

THE TEXT

The *SBL Greek New Testament* (SBLGNT) is a new edition of the Greek New Testament, established with the help of earlier editions. In particular, four editions of the Greek New Testament were utilized as primary resources in the process of establishing the SBLGNT. These editions (and their abbreviations) are:

WH   Brooke Foss Westcott and Fenton John Anthony Hort, *The New Testament in the Original Greek,* vol. 1: *Text*; vol. 2: *Introduction* [and] *Appendix* (Cambridge: Macmillan, 1881). This justly famous and widely influential nineteenth-century edition of the Greek New Testament was one of the key texts used in the creation of the original Nestle text[2] and was used as the initial basis of comparison in the creation of the United Bible Societies' *Greek New Testament*.[3]

Treg   Samuel Prideaux Tregelles, *The Greek New Testament, Edited from Ancient Authorities, with their Various Readings in Full, and the Latin Version of Jerome* (London: Bagster; Stewart, 1857–1879). Although the fine edition of Tregelles has been overshadowed by that of his close contemporaries Westcott and Hort, his textual judgments reveal a "consistency of view and breadth of appreciation" of all the available textual evidence not always as evident in the work of his major nineteenth-century

---

[1] This introduction is a reproduction of the existing introduction written by Michael W. Holmes in the SBLGNT.

[2] Eberhard Nestle, *Novum Testamentum Graece* (Stuttgart: Württembergische Bibelanstalt, 1898); cf. the 16th ed. (1936), 38*; cf. also Kurt Aland and Barbara Aland, *The Text of the New Testament* (2nd ed.; trans. E. F. Rhodes; Grand Rapids: Eerdmans; Leiden: Brill, 1989), 19–20.

[3] Kurt Aland, Matthew Black, Bruce M. Metzger, and Allen Wikgren, eds., *The Greek New Testament* (New York: American Bible Society; London: British and Foreign Bible Society; Edinburgh: National Bible Society of Scotland; Amsterdam: Netherlands Bible Society; Stuttgart: Württemberg Bible Society, 1966), v.

colleagues, who display (to varying degrees) a tendency toward a preoccupation with the latest "big discovery" (Ephraemi Rescriptus/04 in the case of Lachmann, Sinaiticus/01 in the case of Tischendorf, and Vaticanus/03 in the case of Westcott and Hort).[4] Tregelles offers a discerning alternative perspective alongside Westcott and Hort.

NIV   Richard J. Goodrich and Albert L. Lukaszewski, *A Reader's Greek New Testament* (Grand Rapids: Zondervan, 2003). This edition presents the Greek text behind the New International Version[5] as reconstructed by Edward Goodrick and John Kohlenberger III.[6] It thus represents the textual choices made by the Committee on Bible Translation, the international group of scholars responsible for the NIV translation. According to its editors, this edition differs from the United Bible Societies/Nestle-Aland editions of the Greek New Testament at 231 places.[7]

RP   *The New Testament in the Original Greek: Byzantine Textform 2005*, compiled and arranged by Maurice A. Robinson and William G. Pierpont (Southborough, Mass.: Chilton, 2005). This edition offers a text that is a reliable representative of the Byzantine textual tradition.

ESTABLISHING THE TEXT

The starting point for the SBLGNT was the edition of Westcott and Hort. First, the WH text was modified to match the orthographic standards of

---

[4] David C. Parker, "The Development of the Critical Text of the Epistle of James: From Lachmann to the *Editio Critica Maior*," in *New Testament Textual Criticism and Exegesis: Festschrift J. Delobel* (ed. A. Denaux; BETL 161; Leuven: Leuven University Press and Peeters, 2002), 329.

[5] *The Holy Bible, New International Version: New Testament* (Grand Rapids: Zondervan, 1973).

[6] A second edition published by the same editors and publisher in 2007 (reviewed and modified by Gordon Fee) presents the Greek text behind the TNIV translation.

[7] Goodrich and Lukaszewski, *A Reader's Greek New Testament*, 10 n. 6.

the SBLGNT (described below). Next, the modified version was compared to the other three primary editions (Treg, NIV, and RP) in order to identify points of agreement and disagreement between them. Where all four editions agreed, the text was tentatively accepted as the text of the SBL edition; points of disagreement were marked for further consideration. The editor then worked systematically through the entire text, giving particular attention to the points of disagreement but examining as well the text where all four editions were in agreement.[8] Where there was disagreement among the four editions, the editor determined which variant to print as the text;[9] occasionally a reading not found in any of the four editions commended itself as the most probable representative of the text and therefore was adopted. Similarly, where all four texts were in agreement, the editor determined whether to accept that reading or to adopt an alternative variant as the text.[10] In this manner, the text of the SBLGNT was established.

A comparison of this new text with the four editions listed above, using as the database the 6,928 variation units recorded in the accompanying apparatus (described below), reveals the following patterns of agreement and difference:

	Agreements	Disagreements
SBL—WH:	6,047	881
SBL—Treg:	5,699	1,229
SBL—NIV:	6,310	618
SBL—RP:	970	5,958

---

[8] For a brief overview of the editor's methodological and historical perspectives with regard to the practice of New Testament textual criticism, see Michael W. Holmes, "Reconstructing the Text of the New Testament," in *The Blackwell Companion to the New Testament* (ed. David E. Aune; Oxford: Wiley-Blackwell, 2010), 77–89.

[9] Or, to put the matter a bit more precisely, which variant most likely represents the form in which the text first began to be copied and to circulate.

[10] In all, there are fifty-six variation units in the SBLGNT where the editor preferred a reading not found in any of the four primary editions. In thirty-eight of those instances, the editor's preferred reading is also read by WHmarg (30x) and/or Tregmarg (2x) and/or NA (10x).

Also interesting is a comparison of agreements of the SBLGNT with one of the four editions against the other three and, vice versa, SBLGNT and the other three against the one:

SBL + WH vs. Treg NIV RP: 99	SBL + Treg NIV RP vs. WH: 365
SBL + Treg vs. WH NIV RP: 28	SBL + WH NIV RP vs. Treg: 150
SBL + NIV vs. WH Treg RP: 59	SBL + WH Treg RP vs. NIV: 103
SBL + RP vs. WH Treg NIV 66	SBL + WH Treg NIV vs. RP: 4,874

ORTHOGRAPHY AND RELATED MATTERS

The orthography of this edition (including accents and breathings[11]) follows that of the Bauer-Danker-Arndt-Gingrich lexicon (BDAG).[12] This includes both text and apparatus: entries in the apparatus generally have been conformed to the orthography of BDAG regardless of the spelling of the source edition.

With regard to elision (e.g., ἀλλ' for ἀλλά), crasis (e.g., κἀγώ for καὶ ἐγώ), movable ν, and the interchange between first aorist and second aorist verb endings, the text of Westcott and Hort has been followed. As

---

[11] Occasionally breathings are as much a matter of interpretation as of lexicography. In agreement with a minority of the membership of the UBS Editorial Committee (see Bruce M. Metzger, *A Textual Commentary on The Greek New Testament* [London: United Bible Societies, 1971], 616 [a discussion of Phil 3:21 not found in the second edition]), the SBLGNT occasionally prints a rough breathing on forms of αὑτός.

[12] *A Greek-English Lexicon of the New Testament and Other Early Christian Literature* (3rd ed., revised and edited by Frederick William Danker; based on the 6th ed. of Walter Bauer's *Griechisch-deutsches Wörterbuch zu den Schriften des Neuen Testaments und der frühchristlichen Literatur*; Chicago: University of Chicago Press, 2000). Thus ἁγνεία, not ἁγνία (so WH), or, e.g., in the case of words with movable ς (cf. BDF §21), ἄχρι, μέχρι, and οὕτως are printed throughout, unless BDAG indicates otherwise (ἄχρις, Gal 3:19 and Heb 3:13; μέχρις, Mark 13:30, Gal 4:19, Heb 12:4; οὕτω, Acts 23:11, Phil 3:17, Heb 12:21, Rev 16:18). A rare exception to the guideline is the adoption of νουμηνίας rather than νεομηνίας in Col 2:16.

in the case of orthography, this guideline generally applies to the apparatus as well as the text.

CAPITALIZATION

Capitalization follows the pattern of the third edition of *The Apostolic Fathers: Greek Texts and English Translations*,[13] which capitalizes (1) the first word of a paragraph; (2) the first word of direct speech; and (3) proper nouns.[14] Occasionally capitalization in a variant reading in the apparatus may follow that of the source edition.

VERSE DIVISION, PUNCTUATION, AND PARAGRAPHING

The verse divisions follow those of the Nestle-Aland/United Bible Societies Greek texts throughout.[15] Differences between editions have not been recorded.

Punctuation generally follows that of Westcott and Hort. Regular exceptions include instances where a textual decision or the adoption of NRSV paragraphing required a corresponding change in punctuation. Where Westcott and Hort employed two consecutive punctuation marks (such as a comma following or preceding a dash; see 1 Tim 1:5, 2:7), these have been reduced to a single mark. A high point has been added before direct speech if no other punctuation is present. Occasionally other changes have been made as required by context.

Paragraphing generally follows the pattern of the NRSV. Conflicts between NRSV paragraphing and Westcott and Hort punctuation have

---

[13] Michael W. Holmes, ed., *The Apostolic Fathers: Greek Texts and English Translations* (3rd ed.; Grand Rapids: Baker Academic, 2007).

[14] A category that offers, to be sure, numerous opportunities for differences of opinion.

[15] A partial exception occurs at the end of Acts 19, where (in accordance with some editions and many recent translations) a forty-first verse number has been placed in the text, but in brackets ([41]), to indicate uncertainty regarding its status.

been resolved on a contextual basis.¹⁶

SYMBOLS USED IN THE TEXT

⌜ or ⌝ or ⌜¹   A textual note pertains to the following word. When identical words in the same verse are marked, the dotted bracket designates the second occurrence. Third (and subsequent) instances are denoted by a numbered bracket to distinguish them from previous instances.

⌜ ⌝ or ⌜ ⌝¹   A textual note pertains to the enclosed words. When identical phrases in the same verse are marked, dotted brackets designate the second occurrence. Similarly, when a second multiword variation unit falls within the boundaries of a longer multiword variation unit, the dotted brackets mark the second occurrence.

[ ]   The enclosed text is doubtful.¹⁷

---

¹⁶ For example, at the end of Phil 1:18, WH's punctuation was given preference over the NRSV paragraph break, whereas at Phil 2:14 the NRSV paragraphing was followed rather than the WH punctuation (which was changed accordingly).

¹⁷ Brackets have been employed in this edition sparingly—not, one hopes, due to a lack of what Parker nicely terms "wise reticence" in the face of difficult choices (Parker, "Development," 325), but for positive reasons. These include a widely shared sense that brackets have been somewhat overused in some recent editions (sometimes as what could be perceived as a means of avoiding difficult choices); an opinion that one of an editor's duties is to make choices, particularly in the "hard cases," so as to offer some degree of guidance to those making use of the resulting text; and a corresponding concern that the availability of brackets biases the decision-making process toward inclusion (one can bracket an included word about which one has some degree of doubt regarding the decision to include it, but one cannot bracket the omission of a word about which one has an equal degree of doubt regarding the decision to exclude it). In all, for better or worse, single brackets appear only six times in the SBLGNT (at Luke 22:19–20; 24:40; 24:51; 24:52; Eph 1:1; Col 1:20).

The Apparatus

The textual apparatus provides information about a wide range of textual variants.[18] It records all differences between the text of the SBLGNT and the texts of WH, Treg, NIV, RP, and NA except for those differences that fall in the category of "orthography and related matters" (discussed above).[19] That is, the apparatus does not take note of differences that are solely a matter of orthographic variation or that involve only elision, crasis, movable ν, interchange between first and second aorist verb endings, and the like; it does record all other differences between the SBL text and the texts of the five other editions just listed.

The four primary editions (WH Treg NIV RP) are cited for every variation unit (of which there are 6,928).[20] NA is cited only when it differs from NIV. Occasionally a marginal reading of WH or Treg or the text of another edition is cited, usually in support of a reading adopted by the editor that is not found in any of the four primary editions, but sometimes in other circumstances as well.

In each note, the reading of the text is always presented first, in bold, followed by its supporting evidence; the variant reading(s) and supporting evidence follow. Because the different editions use single brackets ([ ]) in the text in different ways, the apparatus does not record details regarding an edition's use of brackets in its text.

Symbols Used in the Notes

•	Separates multiple variation units within a verse.
]	Separates the reading of the text (and its support) from variant readings.

---

[18] In general, it closely follows the pattern of the apparatus in Holmes, *The Apostolic Fathers* (3rd ed.).

[19] This means that the apparatus includes nearly all the variant or alternative readings noted in the margins or notes of most recent major English translations and numerous translations into other languages as well.

[20] For variants involving the verses or parts of verses that WH print between double brackets (⟦ ⟧), WH is cited in the apparatus between brackets (i.e., ⟦WH⟧).

;	Separates multiple variants within a single variation unit.
+	The following text is added by the listed witness(es).
–	The indicated text is omitted by the listed witness(es).
⟦ ⟧	Used by Westcott and Hort to mark material that they did not think belonged to the genuine text but that they did not feel free to remove completely from their printed text due to its antiquity or intrinsic interest. When placed around their initials in the apparatus (i.e., ⟦WH⟧), double brackets signal that WH placed them around the text or variant reading in question.
…	Replaces identical text shared by all the variants in a particular variation unit.

Abbreviations Used in the Notes

ECM	*Novum Testamentum Graecum: Editio Critica Maior*, ed. The Institute for New Testament Textual Research, vol. 4: *Catholic Letters*, ed. Barbara Aland, Kurt Aland, Gerd Mink, Holger Strutwolf, and Klaus Wachtel (4 installments; Stuttgart: Deutsche Biblegesellschaft, 1997–2005): inst. 1: *James* (1997; 2nd rev. impr., 1998); inst. 2: *The Letters of Peter* (2000); inst. 3: *The First Letter of John* (2003); inst. 4: *The Second and Third Letter of John, The Letter of Jude* (2005).
em	emendation
Greeven	Indicates a reading printed as the text by Heinrich Greeven in Albert Huck, *Synopse der drei ersten Evangelien/Synopsis of the First Three Gospels* (13th ed. fundamentally revised by Heinrich Greeven; Tübingen: Mohr Siebeck), 1981).

Holmes	Indicates a reading preferred by the editor that is not found in any of the four primary editions.
NA	Represents the NA$^{26-27}$/UBS$^{3-4}$ editions, which all print the identical Greek text. NA is explicitly cited only when it differs from NIV.
NIV	Richard J. Goodrich and Albert L. Lukaszewski, eds., *A Reader's Greek New Testament* (Grand Rapids: Zondervan, 2003).
RP	*The New Testament in the Original Greek: Byzantine Textform 2005*, compiled and arranged by Maurice A. Robinson and William G. Pierpont (Southborough, Mass.: Chilton, 2005).
TR	*Textus Receptus* ("Received Text"). The phrase technically designates the edition of the Greek New Testament printed by the Elziver Brothers in 1633; in generic use it can designate not only the Elziver text but also its precursors (Erasmus, Stephanus, and Beza) or any similar text.[21]
Treg	Samuel Prideaux Tregelles, *The Greek New Testament, Edited from Ancient Authorities, with their Various Readings in Full, and the Latin Version of Jerome* (London: Bagster; Stewart, 1857–1879).
Treg^{marg}	Indicates a reading printed by Tregelles in the margin of his edition.

---

[21] For example, F. H. A. Scrivener, ed., *Η ΚΑΙΝΗ ΔΙΑΘΗΚΗ, Novum Testamentum: Textus Stephanici A.D. 1550* (4th ed., corrected by E. Nestle; London: Bell; Cambridge: Deighton, Bell, 1906) (the printing of the TR consulted for this edition).

WH	Brooke Foss Westcott and Fenton John Anthony Hort, *The New Testament in the Original Greek*, vol. 1: *Text*; vol. 2: *Introduction* [and] *Appendix* (Cambridge: Macmillan, 1881).
WH[app]	Indicates a reading discussed by WH in the *Appendix* to their edition (in vol. 2).
WH[marg]	Indicates an alternative reading printed by WH in the margin of their edition.

UNDERSTANDING THE APPARATUS: A BRIEF GUIDE

This brief guide supplements what is said above about the apparatus to the SBLGNT by offering further explanation and examples.

The textual apparatus provides a textual note for each of the more than 6,900 instances of variation in the SBLGNT. In each note, the marked reading in the text is always listed first, in bold, and followed immediately by its supporting evidence. The separator bracket (]) comes next, followed by the variant reading(s) and supporting evidence. Multiple variation units in the same verse are separated by a bullet (•), as in all three examples below. Multiple variant readings in the same variation unit are separated by a semicolon (;), as in the second variant in Matt 22:30 below (τοῦ θεοῦ RP; – WH Treg NIV).

Symbols in the text alert the reader to the presence of textual notes in the apparatus. The most frequently used symbols are ⌜ and ⌞ ⌟; the former marks a single word, and the latter encloses a multiple word phrase. If the same word is marked a second time in the same verse, the ⌜ symbol is used to mark the second occurrence (as in Matt 10:28 below, twice). If an identical multiword phrase is marked a second time in the same verse, the ⌞ ⌟ symbols are used to mark the second occurrence (as in John 18:39 below). In both cases, for clarity the symbols are repeated in the textual note. (More complex cases are discussed below.)

INTRODUCTION TO THE SBLGNT

Matt 10:28 text:

28 καὶ μὴ ⌜φοβεῖσθε ἀπὸ τῶν ἀποκτεννόντων τὸ σῶμα τὴν δὲ ψυχὴν μὴ δυναμένων ἀποκτεῖναι· ⌜φοβεῖσθε δὲ μᾶλλον τὸν δυνάμενον ⌜καὶ ψυχὴν ⌜καὶ σῶμα ἀπολέσαι ἐν γεέννῃ.

textual note in apparatus:

28 ⌜**φοβεῖσθε** Treg NIV RP] φοβηθῆτε WH • ⌜**φοβεῖσθε** WH NIV] φοβήθητε Treg RP • ⌜**καὶ** WH Treg NIV] + τὴν RP • ⌜**καὶ** WH Treg NIV] + τὸ RP

John 18:39 text:

39 ἔστιν δὲ συνήθεια ὑμῖν ἵνα ἕνα ⌜ἀπολύσω ὑμῖν⌝ ἐν τῷ πάσχα· βούλεσθε οὖν ⌜ἀπολύσω ὑμῖν⌝ τὸν βασιλέα τῶν Ἰουδαίων;

textual note in apparatus:

39 ⌜**ἀπολύσω ὑμῖν**⌝ WH Treg NIV] ὑμῖν ἀπολύσω RP • ⌜**ἀπολύσω ὑμῖν**⌝ WH Treg NIV] ὑμῖν ἀπολύσω RP

Matt 22:30 text:

30 ἐν γὰρ τῇ ἀναστάσει οὔτε γαμοῦσιν οὔτε ⌜γαμίζονται, ἀλλ' ὡς ἄγγελοι ⌜θεοῦ ἐν ⌜τῷ οὐρανῷ εἰσιν·

textual note in apparatus:

30 ⌜**γαμίζονται** WH Treg NIV] ἐκγαμίζονται RP • **θεοῦ** Holmes] τοῦ θεοῦ RP; – WH Treg NIV • **τῷ** WH Treg NIV] – RP

Variant readings can be one of three types: addition, omission, or substitution. An addition is signaled by the plus sign (+), which indicates that the following word or words are added to the reading of the text by the supporting edition(s) listed after the additional words. In Matt 10:28 above, for example, taking the third and fourth variants together, the SBL

17

text reads καὶ ψυχὴν καὶ σῶμα (with WH Treg NIV), while the RP text—adding τὴν after ⌜καὶ and τὸ after ⌜καὶ —reads καὶ τὴν ψυχὴν καὶ τὸ σῶμα.

An omission is signaled by the minus sign (–) or dash, which indicates that the word(s) marked in the text are omitted by the supporting edition(s) listed after the minus sign. In the second variant in Matt 22:30 above, where the SBL text reads ὡς ἄγγελοι θεοῦ, WH Treg NIV omit the word θεοῦ, and thus read only ὡς ἄγγελοι (see also the last variant in 22:30).

If there is neither a plus nor a minus sign, the variant reading is a substitution: the word(s) marked in the text are replaced by the word(s) in the variant reading by the supporting edition(s) listed after the variant reading. In the first variant in Matt 10:28, for example, the SBL text reads φοβεῖσθε (with Treg NIV RP), while the WH text reads φοβηθῆτε (see also the second variant in this verse, both variants in John 18:39, and the first variant in 22:30).

The above examples cover a very large proportion of the variation units in the apparatus, though more complex cases do sometimes occur. If, for example, the same word is marked more than twice in the same sentence, the symbols ⌜¹ and ⌜² are used for subsequent occurrences (as in 1 Cor 12:10 below, where the same word is marked four times). Occasionally, the ⌞ ⌟ symbols (whose typical use was described above) can also be used to mark a shorter multiword variant that occurs inside a longer multiword variant (see Luke 22:43–44 below). Also, a single-word variant marker (⌜) can occur inside a regular set (⌞ ⌟) of multiple-word variant markers (as in John 13:2 below). A key point to remember when encountering an "opening" multiple-word marker, whether ⌞ or ⌜, is to always look for the corresponding "closing" marker (⌟ or ⌝); this will help to avoid confusion.

1 Cor 12:10 text:

    10 ⌜ἄλλῳ ἐνεργήματα δυνάμεων, ⌜ἄλλῳ προφητεία, ⌜¹ἄλλῳ διακρίσεις πνευμάτων, ⌜ἑτέρῳ γένη γλωσσῶν, ⌜²ἄλλῳ ἑρμηνεία γλωσσῶν·

INTRODUCTION TO THE SBLGNT

textual note in apparatus:

10 ⌜ἄλλῳ Holmes] + δὲ WH Treg NIV RP • ⌜ἄλλῳ Treg] + δὲ WH NIV RP • ⌜¹ἄλλῳ Treg] + δὲ WH NIV RP • ἑτέρῳ WH Treg NIV] + δὲ RP • ⌜²ἄλλῳ Holmes] + δὲ WH Treg NIV RP

Luke 22.43–44 text:

43 ⌜ὤφθη δὲ αὐτῷ ἄγγελος ⌜ἀπ' οὐρανοῦ ἐνισχύων αὐτόν. 44 καὶ γενόμενος ἐν ἀγωνίᾳ ἐκτενέστερον προσηύχετο· ⌝καὶ ἐγένετο⌝ ὁ ἱδρὼς αὐτοῦ ὡσεὶ θρόμβοι αἵματος καταβαίνοντες ἐπὶ τὴν γῆν.⌝

textual note in apparatus:

43–44 ὤφθη δὲ ... ἐπὶ τὴν γῆν. Treg NIV RP] ⟦WH⟧ • **ἀπ'** NIV RP] ἀπὸ τοῦ ⟦WH⟧ Treg • **καὶ ἐγένετο** ⟦WH⟧ NIV] ἐγένετο δὲ Treg RP

Here the symbols ⌜ ⌝ mark off a variant involving the inclusion (by Treg NIV RP) or omission (by WH) of verses 43–44. Within that larger variant, a smaller multiword variant marked by ⌜ ⌝ involves a word-order difference. Since the ⌜ "opening" symbol always is matched by a ⌝ "closing" symbol, and the ⌜ symbol always corresponds with ⌝, it is possible to "nest" the two variants without confusion as to where each begins and ends.

This variant offers an opportunity to comment on the use of another symbol, ⟦WH⟧. There are some verses that Westcott and Hort did not think belonged to the genuine text but that they did not feel free to remove completely from their printed text due to its antiquity or intrinsic interest. In the first entry in the apparatus (**ὤφθη δὲ ... ἐπὶ τὴν γῆν.** Treg NIV RP] ⟦WH⟧), the symbol ⟦WH⟧ signals that Westcott and Hort placed verses 43–44 inside double brackets, whereas Treg NIV RP included them in their texts. In the third variant (**καὶ ἐγένετο** ⟦WH⟧ NIV] ἐγένετο δὲ Treg RP), involving a difference in word order, the presence of ⟦WH⟧ signals that Westcott and Hort support the same word order as NIV and reminds us that they did not view the phrase (or the verse of which it is a part) as part of the original text.

John 13.2 text:

2 καὶ δείπνου ⌜γινομένου, τοῦ διαβόλου ἤδη βεβληκότος εἰς τὴν καρδίαν ἵνα παραδοῖ αὐτὸν Ἰούδας Σίμωνος ⌐Ἰσκαριώτου⌐,

textual note in apparatus:

2 **γινομένου** WH Treg NIV] γενομένου RP • **ἵνα παραδοῖ αὐτὸν Ἰούδας Σίμωνος Ἰσκ.** WH Treg NIV] Ἰούδα Σίμωνος Ἰσκ. ἵνα αὐτὸν παραδῷ RP • **Ἰσκαριώτου** NIV RP] Ἰσκαριώτης WH Treg

In this instance, the word-order variation (ἵνα παραδοῖ αὐτὸν Ἰούδας Σίμωνος Ἰσκαριώτου⌐) is unrelated to the separate variant involving the spelling of ⌐Ἰσκαριώτου, so they have been set up as separate variants, the smaller one "nested" inside the larger. The larger variant bounded by the symbols ⌐ ⌐ deals with the word-order variation, while the variant signaled by the ⌐ symbol deals with the spelling variation.

Two other matters call for comment. One is punctuation, which in general is not taken into account in the textual notes. Occasionally, however, a variant may carry with it consequences for how the verse is punctuated. In these cases, punctuation is included in the textual note, as in the second variant in Rev 21:4:

4 **ἐκ** WH Treg NIV] ἀπὸ RP • **ἔτι.** WH] ἔτι, ὅτι Treg NIV RP

Here the inclusion of ὅτι (supported by Treg NIV RP) alters the syntax of the sentence and so requires a change in punctuation, from the full stop of WH to a comma. The textual note, therefore, indicates both the textual variants and the punctuation that corresponds with them.

The other is the use of ellipsis (…) in the textual notes. Sometimes it is used to save space, especially in variants involving word order. In Matt 15:37 (καὶ ἔφαγον πάντες καὶ ἐχορτάσθησαν, καὶ ⌜τὸ περισσεῦον τῶν κλασμάτων ἦραν⌐ ἑπτὰ σπυρίδας πλήρεις), for example, giving the full text of each variant would result in a textual note like this:

INTRODUCTION TO THE SBLGNT

37 τὸ περισσεῦον τῶν κλασμάτων ἦραν WH Treg
NIV] ἦραν τὸ περισσεῦον τῶν κλασμάτων RP

The use of ellipses to replace exactly the same words in each variant results in a shorter note:

37 τὸ ... κλασμάτων ἦραν WH Treg NIV] ἦραν τὸ ... κλασμάτων RP.

In other cases the use of ellipses helps to make clear the places where two or more textual variants actually differ. In Acts 9:31, for example, the entire verse is enclosed by a pair of multiword variant markers (31 ⸂μὲν οὖν ἐκκλησία καθ' ὅλης τῆς Ἰουδαίας καὶ Γαλιλαίας καὶ Σαμαρείας εἶχεν εἰρήνην οἰκοδομουμένη, καὶ πορευομένη τῷ φόβῳ τοῦ κυρίου καὶ τῇ παρακλήσει τοῦ ἁγίου πνεύματος ἐπληθύνετο⸃). The apparatus, however, looks like this:

31 Ἡ ... ἐκκλησία ... εἶχεν ... οἰκοδομουμένη ... πορευομένη ... ἐπληθύνετο WH Treg NIV] Αἱ ... ἐκκλησίαι ... εἶχον ... οἰκοδομούμεναι ... πορευόμεναι ... ἐπληθύνοντο RP

Here the ellipses not only save space but also reveal clearly the places where the variant readings differ and the nature of the variation (singular versus plural).

21

Colossians

ΠΡΟΣ ΚΟΛΟΣΣΑΕΙΣ

ΠΡΟΣ ΚΟΛΟΣΣΑΕΙΣ

Colossians 1

New Vocabulary by Frequency in Chapter
[Occurrences in Book, Chapter, SBLGNT]

φανερόω, *I make known, reveal* [4, 1, 49]
πρό, prep. *before* [1, 1, 47]
θλῖψις, εως, ἡ, *pressure, affliction* [1, 1, 45]
κατοικέω, *I dwell, inhabit* [2, 1, 44]
γενεά, ας, ἡ, *generation* [1, 1, 43]
πάντοτε, adv. *always, at all times* [3, 1, 41]
παρίστημι, *I am present* [2, 2, 41]
εὐχαριστέω, *I thank; give thanks* [3, 2, 38]
ἐχθρός, ἡ, όν, *hostile, enemy* [1, 1, 32]
ὑπομονή, ῆς, ἡ, *patience, endurance* [1, 1, 32]
σκότος, ους, τό, *darkness* [1, 1, 31]
διάκονος, ου, ὁ, *servant* [4, 3, 29]
μυστήριον, ου, τό, *mystery* [4, 2, 28]
σταυρός, ου, ὁ, *cross* [2, 1, 27]
πνευματικός, ἡ, όν, adj. *spiritual* [2, 1, 26]
γέ, encl. *indeed, even* [1, 1, 25]
γνωρίζω, *I make known* [3, 1, 25]
μανθάνω, *I learn* [1, 1, 25]
παρείμι, *I am near, present, arrive* [1, 1, 24]
Τιμόθεος, ου, ὁ, *Timothy* [1, 1, 24]
αὐξάνω, *I cause to grow, increase* [2, 2, 23]
εἰκών, όνος, ἡ, *image* [2, 1, 23]
κοπιάω, *I toil, labor* [1, 1, 23]
πλοῦτος, τό, *riches, wealth* [2, 1, 22]
εὐδοκέω, *I think well, am well pleased, take pleasure* [1, 1, 21]
ἐπίγνωσις, εως, ἡ, *knowledge, full knowledge* [3, 1, 20]
νυνί, adv. *now, at this moment* [2, 1, 20]
κτίσις, εως, ἡ, *creation* [2, 2, 19]
τέλειος, α, ον, adj. *complete, perfect, mature* [2, 1, 19]

COLOSSIANS 1

καταγγέλλω, *I proclaim* [1, 1, 18]
ἄφεσις, εως, ἡ, *forgiveness, remission* [1, 1, 17]
πλήρωμα, τος, τό, *fullness* [2, 1, 17]
ῥύομαι, *I rescue, deliver* [1, 1, 17]
ἐπιμένω, *I continue* [1, 1, 16]
πάθημα, τος, τό, *suffering* [1, 1, 16]
συνιστήμι, *I place together, hold together* [1, 1, 16]
κτίζω, *I create* [3, 2, 15]
παύομαι, from παύω, *I cease* [1, 1, 15]
μακροθυμία, ας, ἡ, *longsuffering, forbearance* [2, 1, 14]
διάνοια, ας, ἡ, *intention, thought, mind* [1, 1, 12]
κλῆρος, ου, ὁ, *lot, allotment, share* [1, 1, 11]
ἀπολύτρωσις, εως, ἡ, *redemption* [1, 1, 10]
σύνδουλος, ου, ὁ, *fellow slave* [2, 1, 10]
οἰκονομία, ας, ἡ, *household management, stewardship, administration* [1, 1, 9]
ὑστέρημα, τος, τό, *deficiency, need, what is lacking* [1, 1, 9]
ἀγωνίζομαι, *I contend for a prize, fight, struggle* [2, 1, 8]
ἄμωμος, ον, adj. *blameless, without blemish* [1, 1, 8]
ἐνέργεια, ας, ἡ, *action, operation, energy* [2, 1, 8]
καρποφορέω, *I bear fruit* [2, 2, 8]
νουθετέω, *I admonish, advise, warn* [2, 1, 8]
πρωτότοκος, ον, adj. *firstborn* [2, 2, 8]
δηλόω, *I make clear, declare, make known* [1, 1, 7]
σύνεσις, εως, ἡ, *understanding* [2, 1, 7]
ἀξίως, adv. *worthily* [1, 1, 6]
ἀνέγκλητος, ον, adj. *above reproach, irreproachable* [1, 1, 5]
ἀόρατος, ον, adj. *invisible, unseen* [1, 1, 5]
θεμελιόω, *I lay a foundation, found, establish* [1, 1, 5]
μεθίστημι, *I remove, change position, transfer* [1, 1, 5]
μερίς, ίδος, ἡ, *part, portion, share* [1, 1, 5]
ἀπόκειμαι, *I lay up, store up, reserve* [1, 1, 4]
ἀποκρύπτω, *I hide, conceal* [1, 1, 4]
κυριότης, ητος, ἡ, *lordship, authority* [1, 1, 4]

ΠΡΟΣ ΚΟΛΟΣΣΑΕΙΣ

ἀποκαταλάσσω, *I reconcile* [2, 2, 3]
ἀπαλλατριόομαι, from ἀπαλλατριόω, *I alienate, estrange* [1, 1, 3]
ἑδραῖος, α, ον, adj. *steadfast, firm* [1, 1, 3]
Ἐπαφρᾶς, *Epaphras* [2, 1, 3]
δυναμόω, *I strengthen, enable* [1, 1, 2]
ἱκανόω, *I make sufficient, make adequate, enable* [1, 1, 2]
ἀνταναπληρόω, *I fill up, complete* [1, 1, 1]
ἀρεσκεία, ας, ἡ, *desire to please* [1, 1, 1]
εἰρηνοποιέω, *I make peace* [1, 1, 1]
Κολοσσαί, ων, ἡ, *Colossae* [1, 1, 1]
μετακινέω, *I move, move away, shift* [1, 1, 1]
ὁρατός, ή, όν, adj. *visible, seen* [1, 1, 1]
προακούω, *I hear before* [1, 1, 1]
πρωτεύω, *I am first, have first place* [1, 1, 1]

ΠΡΟΣ ΚΟΛΟΣΣΑΕΙΣ

1:1 Παῦλος ἀπόστολος[1] ⌐Χριστοῦ Ἰησοῦ¬ διὰ θελήματος θεοῦ[2] καὶ Τιμόθεος[3] ὁ ἀδελφός[4] 2 τοῖς ἐν ⌐Κολοσσαῖς[5] ἁγίοις καὶ πιστοῖς ἀδελφοῖς ἐν Χριστῷ·[6] χάρις ὑμῖν καὶ εἰρήνη[7] ἀπὸ θεοῦ πατρὸς[8] ⌐ἡμῶν.[9] 3 Εὐχαριστοῦμεν[10] τῷ ⌐θεῷ πατρὶ[11] τοῦ κυρίου ἡμῶν Ἰησοῦ Χριστοῦ πάντοτε[12] ⌐περὶ[13] ὑμῶν προσευχόμενοι,[14] 4 ἀκούσαντες[15] τὴν πίστιν ὑμῶν ἐν Χριστῷ Ἰησοῦ καὶ τὴν ἀγάπην ⌐ἣν ἔχετε¬ εἰς πάντας τοὺς ἁγίους 5 διὰ τὴν ἐλπίδα τὴν ἀποκειμένην[16] ὑμῖν ἐν τοῖς

---

1 TH: ἀπόστολος app. to Παῦλος.
2 TH: subjective gen.
3 Παῦλος...καὶ Τιμόθεος, TH: nom. abs. with "writing" implied, *Paul ... and Timothy (writing)*.
4 TH: ὁ ἀδελφός app. to Τιμόθεος.
5 Κολοσσαί, ων, αἱ, *Colossae*. Pl. by ancient convention.
6 τοῖς ἐν Κολοσσαῖς...ἐν Χριστῷ, TH: dat. of recipients. NA²⁸ indicates some MSS read Ἰησοῦ.
7 χάρις ὑμῖν καὶ εἰρήνη, TH: nom. abs.
8 TH: πατρὸς app. to θεοῦ.
9 NA²⁸ indicates some MSS add καὶ κυρίου Ἰησοῦ Χριστοῦ or καὶ Ἰησοῦ Χριστοῦ τοῦ κυρίου ἡμῶν.
10 εὐχαριστέω, *I thank; give thanks*.
11 TH: πατρὶ app. to θεῷ. NA²⁸ says some MSS read θεῷ καὶ πατρὶ.
12 πάντοτε, adv. *always, at all times*. TH: probably modifying προσευχόμενοι.
13 NA²⁸ indicates some MSS read ὑπὲρ.
14 MH: pres. mid. nom. prtc. pl. of προσεύχομαι. TH: *praying*.
15 TH: *having heard*.
16 ἀπόκειμαι, *I lay up, store up, reserve*, MH: pres. pass. prtc. acc. fem. sg. = root + pass. prtc. morpheme + sg. case ending (ἀποκει + μενη + ν). TH: attrib. with τὴν ἐλπίδα.

27

ΠΡΟΣ ΚΟΛΟΣΣΑΕΙΣ

οὐρανοῖς, ἣν προηκούσατε¹ ἐν τῷ λόγῳ τῆς ἀληθείας τοῦ εὐαγγελίου² 6 τοῦ παρόντος³ εἰς ὑμᾶς, καθὼς καὶ⁴ ἐν παντὶ τῷ ⌜κόσμῳ⁵ ἐστὶν καρποφορούμενον⁶ καὶ αὐξανόμενον⁷ καθὼς καὶ⁸ ἐν ὑμῖν, ἀφ' ἧς ἡμέρας ἠκούσατε καὶ ἐπέγνωτε⁹ τὴν χάριν τοῦ θεοῦ ἐν ἀληθείᾳ· 7 ⌜καθὼς¹⁰ ἐμάθετε¹¹ ἀπὸ Ἐπαφρᾶ¹² τοῦ ἀγαπητοῦ συνδούλου¹³ ἡμῶν, ὅς ἐστιν πιστὸς ὑπὲρ ⌜ἡμῶν¹⁴ διάκονος¹⁵ τοῦ Χριστοῦ, 8 ὁ καὶ¹⁶ δηλώσας¹⁷ ἡμῖν τὴν ὑμῶν ἀγάπην ἐν πνεύματι.

---

1 προακούω, *I hear before*.
2 TH: τοῦ εὐαγγελίου app. to τῷ λόγῳ τῆς ἀληθείας.
3 πάρειμι, *I am near, present, arrive*. MH: pres. act. prtc. gen. neut. sg., TH: attrib., *which has come to you*.
4 TH: ascensive or additive καί, *also, even*.
5 NA²⁸ indicates some MSS read τῷ κόσμῳ καὶ.
6 καρποφορέω, *I bear fruit*. MH: pres. mid. prtc. nom. neut. sg. = root + connecting vowel + mid./pass. prtc. morpheme + neut. sg. case ending (καρποφορ + ου + μενο + ν). TH: periphr. prtc.
7 αὐξάνω, *I cause to grow, increase*. MH: pres. pass. prtc. nom. neut. sg. TH: cmpd. periphr. prtc.
8 TH: ascensive or additive καί, *also, even*.
9 ἐπιγινώσκω, *I know, recognize*. 2nd aor. verb.
10 NA²⁸ indicates some MSS read καθὼς καὶ.
11 μανθάνω, *I learn*. 2nd aor. verb.
12 Ἐπαφρᾶς, ᾶ, ὁ, *Epaphras*.
13 σύνδουλος, ου, ὁ, *fellow slave*. cmpd. TH: τοῦ ἀγαπητοῦ συνδούλου is in app. to Ἐπαφρᾶ.
14 NA²⁸ has ὑπὲρ ὑμῶν, *on your behalf*. There is MS support for ἡμῶν, but it might occur by attraction to the preceding and following 1ˢᵗ per. pl. pron.
15 διάκονος, ου, ὁ, *servant*. TH: πιστὸς ὑπὲρ ἡμῶν διάκονος, pred. nom. with attrib. adj. πιστός.
16 TH: ascensive or additive καί, *also, even*.
17 δηλόω, *I make clear, declare, make known*. MH: aor. act. prtc. nom. masc. sg. TH: subs. prtc. in app. to διάκονος, *the one making clear your love for us in (the) spirit*.

COLOSSIANS 1

9 Διὰ τοῦτο¹ καὶ² ἡμεῖς, ἀφ' ἧς ἡμέρας ἠκούσαμεν, οὐ παυόμεθα³ ὑπὲρ ὑμῶν προσευχόμενοι καὶ αἰτούμενοι⁴ ἵνα⁵ πληρωθῆτε⁶ τὴν ἐπίγνωσιν⁷ τοῦ θελήματος αὐτοῦ ἐν πάσῃ σοφίᾳ καὶ συνέσει⁸ πνευματικῇ⁹, 10 ⸀περιπατῆσαι¹⁰ ἀξίως¹¹ τοῦ κυρίου εἰς πᾶσαν ἀρεσκείαν¹² ἐν παντὶ ἔργῳ ἀγαθῷ καρποφοροῦντες¹³ καὶ αὐξανόμενοι¹⁴ ⸀τῇ ἐπιγνώσει¹⁵⸃ τοῦ θεοῦ, 11 ἐν πάσῃ δυνάμει δυναμούμενοι¹⁶ κατὰ τὸ κράτος¹⁷ τῆς δόξης αὐτοῦ εἰς πᾶσαν ὑπομονὴν¹⁸ καὶ μακροθυμίαν¹⁹ μετὰ χαρᾶς,

---

1 TH: causal, *on account of this*.
2 TH: ascensive or additive καί, *also, even*.
3 παύω, *I cause to cease;* mid. *I cease.* MH: pres. mid. ind. 1ˢᵗ pl.
4 TH: παύω (mid.) takes a complementary participle, *we do not cease praying and asking*.
5 TH: indicates content and goal of the praying.
6 MH: aor. pass. subj. 2ⁿᵈ pl. TH: The acc. dir. obj. is retained with this passive verb, *you would be filled with....*
7 ἐπίγνωσις, εως, ἡ, *knowledge, full knowledge*.
8 σύνεσις, εως, ἡ, *understanding*.
9 πνευματικός, ή, όν, adj. *spiritual*.
10 TH: aor. inf. indicates purpose. NA²⁸ indicates some MSS add ὑμᾶς.
11 ἀξίως, adv. *worthily*.
12 ἀρεσκεία, ας, ἡ, *desire to please*.
13 καρποφορέω, *I bear fruit*. TH: adv. prtc. of manner.
14 αὐξάνω, *I cause to grow, increase*. TH: adv. prtc. of manner.
15 ἐπίγνωσις, εως, ἡ, *knowledge, full knowledge*. NA²⁸ indicates variant ἐν τῇ ἐπιγνώσει. TH: followed by obj. gen.
16 δυναμόω, *I strengthen, enable*. MH: pres. pass. prtc. nom. masc. pl. = root + connecting vowel + pass. prtc. morpheme + nom. pl. case ending (δυναμ + ου + μενο + οι). TH: adv. prtc. of means, *being strengthened*.
17 κράτος, ους, τό, *strength, might*.
18 ὑπομονή, ῆς, ἡ, *patience, endurance*.
19 μακροθυμία, ας, ἡ, *longsuffering, forbearance*.

ΠΡΟΣ ΚΟΛΟΣΣΑΕΙΣ

12 εὐχαριστοῦντες¹ τῷ πατρὶ τῷ ἱκανώσαντι² ⌜ὑμᾶς³ εἰς τὴν μερίδα⁴ τοῦ κλήρου⁵ τῶν ἁγίων ἐν τῷ φωτί, 13 ὃς ἐρρύσατο⁶ ἡμᾶς ἐκ τῆς ἐξουσίας τοῦ σκότους⁷ καὶ μετέστησεν⁸ εἰς τὴν βασιλείαν τοῦ υἱοῦ τῆς ἀγάπης αὐτοῦ, 14 ἐν ᾧ ἔχομεν τὴν ἀπολύτρωσιν⁹, τὴν ἄφεσιν¹⁰ τῶν ἁμαρτιῶν· 15 ὅς¹¹ ἐστιν εἰκὼν¹² τοῦ θεοῦ τοῦ ἀοράτου¹³, πρωτότοκος¹⁴ πάσης κτίσεως¹⁵, 16 ὅτι ἐν αὐτῷ ἐκτίσθη¹⁶ τὰ ⌜πάντα ἐν τοῖς οὐρανοῖς ⌜καὶ ἐπὶ τῆς

---

1 εὐχαριστέω, *I thank; give thanks*. TH: adv. prtc. of manner.
2 ἱκανόω, *I make sufficient, make adequate, enable*. MH: aor. act. prtc. dat. masc. sg. = root + lengthened connecting vowel + tense formative + prtc. morpheme + dat. sg. case ending (ἱκαν + ώ + σα + ντ + ι). NA²⁸ indicates variant καλέσαντι καὶ ἱκανώσαντι.
3 NA²⁸ indicates some MSS read ἡμᾶς, likely by attraction to ἡμᾶς in verse 13.
4 μερίς, ίδος, ἡ, *part, portion, share*.
5 κλῆρος, ου, ὁ, *lot, allotment, share*. TH: metaph. *land, possession* followed by a poss. gen.
6 ῥύομαι, *I rescue, deliver*. MH: aor. ind. dep. 3ʳᵈ sg. = augment + root + tense formative + per. ending (ἐρ + ρύ + σα + το).
7 σκότος, ους, τό, *darkness*.
8 μεθίστημι, *I remove, change position, transfer*. MH: aor. act. ind. 3ʳᵈ sg = prefix (from μετά) + aug. + root + per. ending (μετ + έ + στη + σεν).
9 ἀπολύτρωσις, εως, ἡ, *redemption*.
10 ἄφεσις, εως, ἡ, *forgiveness, remission*. TH: τὴν ἄφεσιν is app. to τὴν ἀπολύτρωσιν followed by a poss. gen.
11 TH: refers to *the Son* of 1:13.
12 εἰκών, όνος, ἡ, *image*. TH: pred. nom.
13 ἀόρατος, ον, adj. *invisible, unseen*.
14 πρωτότοκος, ον, adj. *firstborn*. TH: in app. to εἰκών referring to *the Son* of 1:13.
15 κτίσις, εως, ἡ, *creation*. TH: πάσης κτίσεως, gen. of ref., with reference to the entire creation, *of all creation*.
16 κτίζω, *I create*. MH: aor. pass. ind. 3ʳᵈ sg. TH: with neut. pl. subject τὰ πάντα.

COLOSSIANS 1

γῆς¹, τὰ ὁρατὰ² καὶ τὰ ἀόρατα³, εἴτε θρόνοι εἴτε κυριότητες⁴ εἴτε ἀρχαὶ εἴτε ἐξουσίαι· τὰ πάντα δι' αὐτοῦ καὶ εἰς αὐτὸν ἔκτισται·⁵ 17 καὶ αὐτός ἐστιν πρὸ⁶ πάντων καὶ τὰ πάντα⁷ ἐν αὐτῷ συνέστηκεν⁸, 18 καὶ αὐτός ἐστιν ἡ κεφαλὴ τοῦ σώματος τῆς ἐκκλησίας⁹· ὅς ⌜ἐστιν ἀρχή¹⁰, πρωτότοκος¹¹ ἐκ τῶν νεκρῶν¹², ἵνα γένηται ἐν πᾶσιν αὐτὸς πρωτεύων¹³, 19 ὅτι ἐν αὐτῷ εὐδόκησεν¹⁴ πᾶν τὸ πλήρωμα¹⁵ κατοικῆσαι¹⁶ 20 καὶ δι' αὐτοῦ ἀποκαταλλάξαι¹⁷ τὰ πάντα εἰς αὐτόν, εἰρηνοποιήσας¹⁸ διὰ τοῦ αἵματος τοῦ σταυροῦ¹⁹ αὐτοῦ, ⌜[δι' αὐτοῦ]²⁰⌝ εἴτε τὰ

---

1 In NA²⁸ some MSS read τὰ ἐν τοῖς οὐρανοῖς καὶ τὰ ἐπὶ τῆς γῆς.
2 ὁρατός, ή, όν, adj. *visible, seen*. TH: in app. to τὰ πάντα.
3 ἀόρατος, ον, adj. *invisible, unseen*. TH: in app. to τὰ πάντα.
4 κυριότης, ητος, ἡ, *lordship, authority*.
5 κτίζω, *I create*. MH: pf. pass. ind. 3ʳᵈ sg.
6 πρό, prep. *before*.
7 TH: nom. subject of 3rd sg. verb συνέστηκεν.
8 συνίστημι, *I place together, hold together*. MH: pf. ind. act. 3ʳᵈ sg.
9 TH: τῆς ἐκκλησίας is in app. to τοῦ σώματος.
10 NA²⁸ indicates some MSS read ἡ ἀρχή. TH: pred. nom.
11 πρωτότοκος, ον, adj. *firstborn*. TH: in app. to ἀρχή.
12 TH: abl. *out of the dead ones*.
13 πρωτεύω, *I am first, have first place*. TH: periphr. prtc. with γένηται.
14 εὐδοκέω, *I think well, am well pleased, take pleasure*.
15 πλήρωμα, τος, τό, *fullness*, TH: referring to God (see Col 2:9) and subject of εὐδόκησεν.
16 κατοικέω, *I dwell, inhabit*. MH: aor. act. inf. TH: complementary infinitive with εὐδόκησεν.
17 ἀποκαταλλάσσω, *I reconcile*. MH: aor. act. inf. TH: complementary infinitive with εὐδόκησεν.
18 εἰρηνοποιέω, *I make peace*. MH: aor. act. prtc. nom. masc. sg.
19 σταυρός, ου, ὁ, *cross*.
20 NA²⁸ indicates some MSS omit δι' αὐτοῦ.

ΠΡΟΣ ΚΟΛΟΣΣΑΕΙΣ

ἐπὶ τῆς γῆς εἴτε τὰ ⌜ἐν τοῖς οὐρανοῖς¹· 21 καὶ ὑμᾶς² ποτε³ ὄντας ἀπηλλοτριωμένους⁴ καὶ ἐχθροὺς⁵ τῇ διανοίᾳ⁶ ἐν τοῖς ἔργοις τοῖς πονηροῖς — 22 νυνὶ⁷ δὲ ⌜ἀποκατηλλάγητε⁸ ἐν τῷ σώματι τῆς σαρκὸς⁹ αὐτοῦ διὰ τοῦ θανάτου — παραστῆσαι¹⁰ ὑμᾶς ἁγίους καὶ ἀμώμους¹¹ καὶ ἀνεγκλήτους¹² κατενώπιον¹³ αὐτοῦ, 23 εἴ γε¹⁴

---

1 TH: the prep. phrases are made into subtantives, *whether the things on the earth, whether things in the heavens.*
2 TH: acc. subject of adv. periphr. constr. (*while/although you were once alienated...*) is connected referentially to the ὑμᾶς in 1:22.
3 ποτέ, adv. *then.* TH: note the ποτέ/νῦν, *then/now* argumentation in 1:21-22.
4 ἀπαλλατριόομαι, *I alienate, estrange.* MH: pf. pass. prtc. acc. masc. pl. TH: periphr. prtc. with ὄντας.
5 ἐχθρός, ή, όν, *hostile, enemy.* TH: pred. adj. with ὄντας describing ὑμᾶς.
6 διάνοια, ας, ἡ, *intention, thought, mind.* TH: dat. of ref. or of sphere, *in (reference to) mind*
7 νυνί, adv. *now, at this moment,* emphatic form of νῦν strengthened by ι demonstrative.
8 ἀποκαταλλάσσω, *I reconcile.* MH: aor. pass. ind. 3rd sg. NA^{28} uses the more strongly attested ἀποκατήλλαξεν (aor. act. ind. 3rd sg.) and indicates variant readings: ἀποκαταλλαγέντες, ἀποκατήλλακται, ἀπήλλαξεν.
9 TH: attrib. gen., *his fleshly body.*
10 παρίστημι, *I am present.* MH: aor. act. inf. TH: inf. of purpose, *you were reconciled (in order) to present you.*
11 ἄμωμος, ον, adj. *blameless, without blemish.* TH: this and other acc. adj. here are complements in double acc. with ὑμᾶς (dir. obj.).
12 ἀνέγκλητος, ον, adj. *above reproach, irreproachable.*
13 κατενώπιον, adv. *in front of, before* (as a prep. takes gen.).
14 γέ, encl. *indeed, even.*

COLOSSIANS 1

ἐπιμένετε¹ τῇ πίστει τεθεμελιωμένοι² καὶ ἑδραῖοι³ καὶ μὴ μετακινούμενοι⁴ ἀπὸ τῆς ἐλπίδος τοῦ εὐαγγελίου οὗ⁵ ἠκούσατε, τοῦ κηρυχθέντος⁶ ἐν ⸀πάσῃ κτίσει⁷ τῇ ὑπὸ τὸν οὐρανόν, οὗ⁸ ἐγενόμην ἐγὼ Παῦλος⁹ διάκονος¹⁰.

24 Νῦν χαίρω ἐν τοῖς παθήμασιν¹¹ ὑπὲρ ὑμῶν, καὶ ἀνταναπληρῶ¹² τὰ ὑστερήματα¹³ τῶν θλίψεων¹⁴ τοῦ Χριστοῦ¹⁵ ἐν τῇ σαρκί μου ὑπὲρ τοῦ σώματος αὐτοῦ, ὅ ἐστιν ἡ ἐκκλησία, 25 ἧς¹⁶ ἐγενόμην ἐγὼ διάκονος¹⁷ κατὰ

---

1 ἐπιμένω, *I continue* (with dat. dir. obj.).
2 θεμελιόω, *I lay a foundation, found, establish*. MH: pf. mid. prtc. nom. masc. pl. = redupl. + root + lengthened contract vowel + mid./pass. prtc. morpheme + nom. pl. case ending (τε + θεμελι + ω + μενο + ι).
3 ἑδραῖος, α, ον, adj. *steadfast, firm*.
4 μετακινέω, *I move, move away, shift*. MH: pres. mid. prtc. nom. masc. pl.
5 TH: gen. rel. pron. is dir. obj. of ἠκούσατε (which can take a gen. dir. obj.).
6 MH: aor. pass. prtc. gen. neut. pl. = root + tense formative + aor. pass. prtc. morpheme + gen. pl. ending (κηρυχ + θε + ντ + ος). TH: in app. to τοῦ εὐαγγελίου οὗ.
7 κτίσις, εως, ἡ, *creation*. TH: followed by the art. τῇ marking attrib. position.
8 TH: poss. gen. referring to τοῦ εὐαγγελίου, *the servant of which I Paul became*.
9 TH: Παῦλος app. to ἐγώ.
10 διάκονος, ου, ὁ, *servant*. TH: pred. nom.
11 πάθημα, τος, τό, *suffering*. NA²⁸ indicates some MSS read τοῖς παθήμασίν μου.
12 ἀνταναπληρόω, *I fill up, complete*.
13 ὑστέρημα, τος, τό, *deficiency, need, what is lacking*.
14 θλῖψις, εως, ἡ, *pressure, affliction*.
15 TH: subjective gen.
16 TH: poss. gen. referring to ἡ ἐκκλησία, *of which I became a servant*.
17 διάκονος, ου, ὁ, *servant*.

ΠΡΟΣ ΚΟΛΟΣΣΑΕΙΣ

τὴν οἰκονομίαν[1] τοῦ θεοῦ τὴν δοθεῖσάν[2] μοι εἰς ὑμᾶς πληρῶσαι[3] τὸν λόγον τοῦ θεοῦ, 26 τὸ μυστήριον[4] τὸ ἀποκεκρυμμένον[5] ἀπὸ τῶν αἰώνων καὶ ἀπὸ τῶν γενεῶν[6],— ⌜νῦν δὲ ἐφανερώθη[7] τοῖς ἁγίοις αὐτοῦ, 27 οἷς ἠθέλησεν ὁ θεὸς γνωρίσαι[8] τί[9] τὸ πλοῦτος[10] τῆς δόξης τοῦ μυστηρίου[11] τούτου ἐν τοῖς ἔθνεσιν, ⌜ὅ ἐστιν Χριστὸς ἐν ὑμῖν, ἡ ἐλπὶς[12] τῆς δόξης· 28 ὃν ἡμεῖς καταγγέλλομεν[13] νουθετοῦντες[14] πάντα ἄνθρωπον καὶ διδάσκοντες πάντα ἄνθρωπον ἐν πάσῃ σοφίᾳ, ἵνα

---

1 οἰκονομία, ας, ἡ, *household management, stewardship, administration*. TH: followed by subjective gen.
2 MH: aor. pass. prtc. acc. fem. sg. from δίδωμι = root + prtc. morpheme + fem. tense formative + acc. ending (δο + θει + σα + ν). TH: attrib. prtc. with τὴν οἰκονομίαν.
3 MH: aor. act. inf. TH: inf. of purpose.
4 μυστήριον, ου, τό, *mystery*.
5 ἀποκρύπτω, *I hide, conceal*. MH: pf. pass. prtc. acc. neut. sg. cmpd. = prefix (ἀπο) + redupl. + root + neut. prtc. morpheme + acc. ending (ἀπο + κε + κρυπ + μένο + ν). The final stem consonant π elides with the μ of the prtc. morpheme to form μμ.
6 γενεά, ας, ἡ, *generation*.
7 φανερόω, *I make known, reveal*.
8 γνωρίζω, *I make known*. MH: aor. act. inf. TH: complementary inf. with ἠθέλησεν.
9 TH: begins indir. question with implied verb ἐστίν, *what is....*
10 πλοῦτος, τό, *riches, wealth*.
11 μυστήριον, ου, τό, *mystery*.
12 TH: ἡ ἐλπὶς τῆς δόξης app. to Χριστὸς ἐν ὑμῖν.
13 καταγγέλλω, *I proclaim*.
14 νουθετέω, *I admonish, advise, warn*.

COLOSSIANS 1

παραστήσωμεν¹ πάντα ἄνθρωπον τέλειον² ἐν ⸂Χριστῷ⸃³· 29 εἰς ὃ καὶ⁴ κοπιῶ⁵ ἀγωνιζόμενος⁶ κατὰ τὴν ἐνέργειαν⁷ αὐτοῦ τὴν ἐνεργουμένην⁸ ἐν ἐμοὶ ἐν δυνάμει.

---

1 παρίστημι, *I am present.*
2 τέλειος, α, ον, adj. *complete, perfect, mature.* TH: double acc. πάντα ἄνθρωπον (dir. obj.), τέλειον (complement).
3 NA²⁸ indicates some MSS read Χριστῷ Ἰησοῦ.
4 TH: ascensive or additive καί, *also, even.*
5 κοπιάω, *I toil, labor.*
6 ἀγωνίζομαι, *I contend for a prize, fight, struggle.*
7 ἐνέργεια, ας, ἡ, *action, operation, energy.* TH: followed by subjective gen., *his working.*
8 TH: attrib. prtc. in 2nd attrib. position with τὴν ἐνέργειαν.

ΠΡΟΣ ΚΟΛΟΣΣΑΕΙΣ

Colossians 2

New Vocabulary by Frequency in Chapter
[Occurrences in Book, Chapter, SBLGNT]

παραλαμβάνω, I receive, take [2, 1, 49]
κρατέω, I take hold of, grasp [1, 1, 47]
κατοικέω, I dwell, inhabit [2, 1, 44]
μέρος, ους, τό, part [1, 1, 42]
τιμή, ης, ἡ, honor, price, value [1, 1, 41]
ἅπτω, I touch, handle [1, 1, 39]
περισσεύω, I abound, exceed, surpass [1, 1, 39]
περιτομή, ῆς, ἡ, circumcision [4, 2, 36]
παρρησία, ας, ἡ, boldness [1, 1, 31]
γνῶσις, εως, ἡ, wisdom, knowledge [1, 1, 29]
μυστήριον, ου, τό, mystery [4, 1, 28]
σταυρός, ου, ὁ, cross [2, 1, 27]
ἑορτή, ης, ἡ, feast, festival [1, 1, 25]
νοῦς, νοός, ὁ, mind, intellect [1, 1, 24]
αὐξάνω, I cause to grow, increase [2, 1, 23]
χαρίζομαι, I give freely, forgive [2, 1, 23]
πλοῦτος, τό, riches, wealth [2, 1, 22]
διδασκαλία, ας, ἡ, teaching [1, 1, 21]
ἀκροβυστία, ας, ἡ, uncircumcised, foreskin [2, 1, 20]
ἐπίγνωσις, εως, ἡ, knowledge, full knowledge [3, 1, 20]
παράπτωμα, τος, τό, trespass [1, 1, 19]
κενός, ή, όν, adj. empty [1, 1, 18]
θησαυρός, ου, ὁ, treasure [1, 1, 17]
περιτέμνω, I circumcise [1, 1, 17]
πλήρωμα, fullness [2, 1, 17]
γεύομαι, I taste [1, 1, 15]
εὐχαριστία, ας, ἡ, thanksgiving [2, 1, 15]
παράδοσις, εως, ἡ, tradition [1, 1, 13]

COLOSSIANS 2

βρῶσις, εως, ἡ, *food, eating* [1, 1, 11]
τάξις, εως, ἡ, *arrangement, order* [1, 1, 9]
φθορά, ᾶς, ἡ, *destruction, ruin, decay* [1, 1, 9]
βεβαιόω, *I confirm, secure, establish* [1, 1, 8]
ἐνέργεια, ας, ἡ, *action, operation, energy* [2, 1, 8]
ἀπάτη, ης, ἡ, *deceit, deceitfulness* [1, 1, 7]
ἐποικοδομέω, *I build on, build up* [1, 1, 7]
σκιά, ᾶς, ἡ, *shadow* [1, 1, 7]
στοιχεῖον, ου, τό, *element* [1, 1, 7]
συμβιβάζω, *I put together, unite* [2, 2, 7]
σύνεσις, εως, ἡ, *understanding* [2, 1, 7]
ταπεινοφροσύνη, ης, ἡ, *humility* [2, 1, 7]
φυσιόω, *I puff up* [1, 1, 7]
ἀγών, ῶνος, ὁ, *struggle, fight* [1, 1, 6]
εἰκῇ, adv. *without cause, without reason* [1, 1, 6]
Λαοδίκεια, ας, ἡ, *Laodicea* [4, 1, 6]
δόγμα, τος, τό, *decree, ordinance* [1, 1, 5]
ἐξαλείφω, *I wipe out, erase, obliterate* [1, 1, 5]
ἐπιχορηγέω, *I furnish, supply* [1, 1, 5]
βαπτισμός, οῦ, ὁ, *baptism, immersion, dipping* [1, 1, 4]
θρησκεία, ας, ἡ, *religion, worship* [1, 1, 4]
πληροφορία, ας, ἡ, *full assurance, certainty* [1, 1, 4]
σύνδεσμος, ου, ὁ, *bond, link, sinew* [2, 1, 4]
ἀπόκρυφος, ον, adj. *hidden, secret* [1, 1, 3]
ἀχειροποίητος, ον, *not hand made* [1, 1, 3]
ἔνταλμα, τος, τό, *command, commandment* [1, 1, 3]
ἡλίκος, η, ον, adj. *how great, how much* [1, 1, 3]
θιγγάνω, *I touch* [1, 1, 3]
πόσις, εως, ἡ, *drink, drinking* [1, 1, 3]
συνεγείρω, *raise with, raise up with* [2, 1, 3]
ἀπεκδύομαι, *I remove, strip off, undress* [2, 1, 2]
αὔξησις, *growth, increase* [1, 1, 2]
ἁφή, ῆς, ἡ, *ligament* [1, 1, 2]
δειγματίζω, *I disgrace, expose, make a show of* [1, 1, 2]

ΠΡΟΣ ΚΟΛΟΣΣΑΕΙΣ

θριαμβεύω, *I triumph over, lead in triumphal procession* [1, 1, 2]
παραλογίζομαι, *I deceive, delude* [1, 1, 2]
προσηλόω, *I nail, fasten with nails, pin* [1, 1, 1]
ῥιζόομαι, from ῥιζόω, *I root, take root* [1, 1, 2]
συζωοποιέω, *I make alive with* [1, 1, 2]
συνθάπτομαι, from συνθάπτω, *I bury with, bury together* [1, 1, 2]
ὑπεναντίος, α, ον, adj. *opposed, contrary* [1, 1, 2]
ἄπειμι, *I am absent, go away, depart* [1, 1, 1]
ἀπέκδυσις, εως, ἡ, *removal, stripping off* [1, 1, 1]
ἀπόχρησις, εως, ἡ, *use, using up* [1, 1, 1]
ἀφειδία, ας, ἡ, *harsh treatment* [1, 1, 1]
δογματίζομαι, from δογματίζω, *I decree,* [1, 1, 1]
ἐμβατεύω, *I enter in* [1, 1, 1]
ἐθελοθρησκία, ας, ἡ, *self-made religion, self-made worship* [1, 1, 1]
θεότης, ητος, ἡ, *deity* [1, 1, 1]
καταβραβεύω, *I decide against, disqualify* [1, 1, 1]
νεομηνία, ας, ἡ, *new moon, first of the month* [1, 1, 1]
πιθανολογία, ας, ἡ, *persuasive speech* [1, 1, 1]
πλησμονή, *fullness, satisfaction, indulgence* [1, 1, 1]
στερέωμα, τος, τό, *firmness* [1, 1, 1]
συλαγωγέω, *I take captive* [1, 1, 1]
σωματικῶς, adv. *bodily* [1, 1, 1]
χειρόγραφον, ου, τό, *hand written, record of debt* [1, 1, 1]
φιλοσοφία, ας, ἡ, *philosophy* [1, 1, 1]

2:1 Θέλω γὰρ ὑμᾶς εἰδέναι ἡλίκον¹ ἀγῶνα² ἔχω ⌜ὑπὲρ ὑμῶν³ καὶ τῶν ἐν Λαοδικείᾳ⁴ καὶ ὅσοι οὐχ ἑόρακαν⁵ τὸ πρόσωπόν μου ἐν σαρκί⁶, 2 ἵνα παρακληθῶσιν αἱ καρδίαι αὐτῶν, ⌜συμβιβασθέντες⁷ ἐν ἀγάπῃ καὶ εἰς ⌜πᾶν πλοῦτος⁸⌝ τῆς πληροφορίας⁹ τῆς συνέσεως¹⁰, εἰς ἐπίγνωσιν¹¹ τοῦ μυστηρίου¹² τοῦ ⌜θεοῦ, Χριστοῦ¹³, 3 ἐν ᾧ εἰσιν πάντες οἱ θησαυροὶ¹⁴ τῆς σοφίας ⌜καὶ γνώσεως¹⁵ ἀπόκρυφοι¹⁶. 4 ⌜τοῦτο λέγω ἵνα ⌜μηδεὶς ὑμᾶς

---

1 ἡλίκος, η, ον, adj. *how great, how much*. TH: a measure of size or intensity; begins an indir. question.
2 ἀγών, ῶνος, ὁ, *struggle, fight*.
3 NA²⁸ indicates some MSS read περὶ ὑμῶν.
4 Λαοδίκεια, ας, ἡ, *Laodicea*. NA²⁸ indicates some MSS add καὶ τῶν ἐν Ἱεραπόλει, as in 4:13.
5 MH: pf. act. ind. 3rd pl. from ὁράω. = redupl. + root + tense formative + 3ʳᵈ pl. ending (ἑ + ορα + κα + ν).
6 TH: idiomatic, *in person*.
7 συμβιβάζω, *I put together, unite*. MH: aor. pass. prtc. nom. masc. pl., = root + aor. pass. tense formative + aor. pass. prtc. morpheme + nom. ending (συμβιβασ + θε + ντ + ες). Stem consonant ζ elides to become σ. Does not agree with nom. fem. subject αἱ καρδίαι, but to the implied referent "you" (masc. default). NA²⁸ indicates variant readings: συμβιβασθέντων, συμβιβασθῶσιν.
8 πλοῦτος, τό, *riches, wealth*. NA²⁸ indicates variant πᾶν τὸ πλοῦτος.
9 πληροφορία, ας, ἡ, *full assurance, certainty*.
10 σύνεσις, εως, ἡ, *understanding*.
11 ἐπίγνωσις, εως, ἡ, *knowledge, full knowledge*.
12 μυστήριον, ου, τό, *mystery*.
13 TH: Χριστοῦ app. to τοῦ μυστηρίου. NA²⁸ indicates a range of variant readings.
14 θησαυρός, ου, ὁ, *treasure*.
15 γνῶσις, εως, ἡ, *wisdom, knowledge*. TH: τῆς σοφίας καὶ γνώσεως gen. of content.
16 ἀπόκρυφος, ον, adj. *hidden, secret*. TH: pred. adj.

ΠΡΟΣ ΚΟΛΟΣΣΑΕΙΣ

παραλογίζηται[1] ἐν πιθανολογίᾳ[2]. 5 εἰ γὰρ καί[3] τῇ σαρκί[4] ἄπειμι[5], ἀλλὰ τῷ πνεύματι σὺν ὑμῖν εἰμι, χαίρων καὶ βλέπων ὑμῶν τὴν τάξιν[6] καὶ τὸ στερέωμα[7] τῆς εἰς Χριστὸν[8] πίστεως ὑμῶν.

6 Ὡς οὖν παρελάβετε[9] τὸν Χριστὸν Ἰησοῦν τὸν κύριον[10], ἐν αὐτῷ περιπατεῖτε, 7 ἐρριζωμένοι[11] καὶ ἐποικοδομούμενοι[12] ἐν αὐτῷ καὶ ⌜βεβαιούμενοι[13] τῇ πίστει καθὼς ἐδιδάχθητε[14], ⌜περισσεύοντες[15] ἐν εὐχαριστίᾳ[16].

8 Βλέπετε[17] μή τις ὑμᾶς ἔσται ὁ συλαγωγῶν[18] διὰ

---

1 παραλογίζομαι, *I deceive, delude*. ΜΗ: pres. mid. subj. 3rd sg.
2 πιθανολογία, ας, ἡ, *persuasive speech*.
3 TH: ascensive or additive καί, *also, even*.
4 TH: idiomatic, *in person*.
5 ἄπειμι, *I am absent, go away, depart*.
6 τάξις, εως, ἡ, *arrangement, order*.
7 στερέωμα, τος, τό, *firmness*.
8 TH: εἰς Χριστὸν, expresses the dir. obj. of the verbal notion in πίστεως.
9 παραλαμβάνω, *I receive, take*.
10 TH: τὸν κύριον is in app. to τὸν Χριστὸν Ἰησοῦν.
11 ῥιζόω, *I root, take root*. ΜΗ: pf. mid. prtc. nom. masc. pl. = redupl. + root + prtc. morpheme + nom. pl. ending (ἐρ + ριζω + μενο + ι). Stem vowel ο lengthens to ω. TH: mid. voice is more likely than pass. because the prtc. modifies the impv. περιπατεῖτε. The letter recipients are themselves to perform the action.
12 ἐποικοδομέω, *I build on, build up*.
13 βεβαιόω, *I confirm, secure, establish*. NA^{28} indicates variant ἐν τῇ πίστει.
14 MH: aor. pass. ind. 2nd pl.
15 περισσεύω, *I abound, exceed, surpass*.
16 εὐχαριστία, ας, ἡ, *thanksgiving*. NA^{28} indicates variants ἐν αὐτῇ ἐν εὐχαριστίᾳ and ἐν αὐτῷ ἐν εὐχαριστίᾳ.
17 TH: impv. verb followed by content clause initiated by μή.
18 συλαγωγέω, *I take captive*. TH: pred. nom. also taking ὑμᾶς as dir. obj., *the one taking you captive*.

COLOSSIANS 2

τῆς φιλοσοφίας[1] καὶ κενῆς[2] ἀπάτης[3] κατὰ τὴν παράδοσιν[4] τῶν ἀνθρώπων[5], κατὰ τὰ στοιχεῖα[6] τοῦ κόσμου καὶ οὐ κατὰ Χριστόν· 9 ὅτι ἐν αὐτῷ κατοικεῖ[7] πᾶν τὸ πλήρωμα[8] τῆς θεότητος[9] σωματικῶς[10], 10 καὶ ἐστὲ ἐν αὐτῷ πεπληρωμένοι[11], ὅς ἐστιν ἡ κεφαλὴ πάσης ἀρχῆς καὶ ἐξουσίας, 11 ἐν ᾧ καὶ[12] περιετμήθητε[13] περιτομῇ[14] ἀχειροποιήτῳ[15] ἐν τῇ ἀπεκδύσει[16] τοῦ ⌜σώματος τῆς σαρκός[17], ἐν τῇ περιτομῇ[18] τοῦ Χριστοῦ, 12 συνταφέντες[19] αὐτῷ ἐν τῷ ⌜βαπτισμῷ[20], ἐν ᾧ καὶ[21]

---

1 φιλοσοφία, ας, ἡ, *philosophy*.
2 κενός, ή, όν, adj. *empty*.
3 ἀπάτη, ης, ἡ, *deceit, deceitfulness*.
4 παράδοσις, εως, ἡ, *tradition*.
5 TH: attrib. gen.
6 στοιχεῖον, ου, τό, *element, element of nature*. TH: occurs only in pl. in the NT, *elemental properties* or *principles*.
7 κατοικέω, *I dwell, inhabit*.
8 πλήρωμα, ατος, τό, *fullness*. TH: nom. subject of κατοικεῖ.
9 θεότης, ητος, ἡ, *deity*. TH: gen. of content.
10 σωματικῶς, adv. *bodily*.
11 MH: pf. pass. prtc. nom. masc. pl. from πληρόω. TH: periphr. prtc.
12 TH: ascensive or additive καί, *also, even*.
13 περιτέμνω, *I circumcise*. TH: cmpd., *cut around*. MH: aor. pass. ind. 2nd pl. = prefix (περι) + aug. + root + aor. pass. tense formative + 2nd ending (περι + ε + τμη + θη + τε).
14 περιτομή, ῆς, ἡ, *circumcision*. TH: dat. of means.
15 ἀχειροποίητος, ον, *not hand made*.
16 ἀπέκδυσις, εως, ἡ, *removal, stripping off*. TH: means.
17 TH: τῆς σαρκός, attrib. gen., *the body of flesh*. NA^{28} indicates variant τοῦ σώματος τῶν ἁμαρτιῶν.
18 περιτομή, ῆς, ἡ, *circumcision*.
19 συνθάπτω, *I bury with, bury together with*. MH: aor. pass. prtc. nom. masc. pl.
20 βαπτισμός, οῦ, ὁ, *baptism, immersion, dipping*. NA^{28} indicates variant βαπτίσματι.
21 TH: ascensive or additive καί, *also, even*.

ΠΡΟΣ ΚΟΛΟΣΣΑΕΙΣ

συνηγέρθητε[1] διὰ τῆς πίστεως τῆς ἐνεργείας[2] τοῦ θεοῦ τοῦ ἐγείραντος[3] αὐτὸν ⌜ἐκ νεκρῶν[4]. 13 καὶ ὑμᾶς νεκροὺς ὄντας[5] ⌜ἐν[6] τοῖς παραπτώμασιν[7] καὶ τῇ ἀκροβυστίᾳ[8] τῆς σαρκὸς ὑμῶν, συνεζωοποίησεν[9] ὑμᾶς[10] σὺν αὐτῷ· χαρισάμενος[11] ἡμῖν πάντα τὰ παραπτώματα[12], 14 ἐξαλείψας[13] τὸ καθ' ἡμῶν χειρόγραφον[14] τοῖς δόγμασιν[15] ὃ ἦν ὑπεναντίον[16] ἡμῖν, καὶ αὐτὸ ἦρκεν[17]

---

1 συνεγείρω, *raise with, raise up with*.
2 ἐνέργεια, ας, ἡ, *action, operation, energy*. TH: followed by subjective gen.
3 MH: aor. act. prtc. gen. masc. sg. from ἐγείρω.
4 NA²⁸ indicates variant τῶν νεκρῶν.
5 TH: adv. prtc. clause yet grammatically linked to the second ὑμᾶς, *while you were dead*.
6 NA²⁸ indicates some MSS do not have ἐν.
7 παράπτωμα, τος, τό, *trespass*.
8 ἀκροβυστία, ας, ἡ, *uncircumcision, foreskin*.
9 συζωοποιέω, *I make alive with*.
10 NA²⁸ indicates some MSS read ἡμᾶς.
11 χαρίζομαι, *I give freely, forgive*. MH: aor. mid. prtc. nom. masc. sg. = root + tense formative + prtc. morpheme + nom. masc. ending (χαρι + σα + μεν + ος).
12 παράπτωμα, τος, τό, *trespass*.
13 ἐξαλείφω, *I wipe out, erase, obliterate*. MH: aor. act. prtc. nom. masc. sg. = root + tense formative + prtc. morpheme + nom. sg. ending (ἐξαλεί + ψα + ς). Stem consonant φ elides with consonant of tense formative σ to form ψ.
14 χειρόγραφον, ου, τό, *hand written, record of debt*. TH: with καθ' ἡμῶν, *the record of debt against us*.
15 δόγμα, τος, τό, *decree, ordinance*. TH: dat. of association, *with decrees*, or dat. of material, *in decrees*.
16 ὑπεναντίος, α, ον, adj. *opposed, contrary*.
17 MH: pf. act. ind. 3ʳᵈ sg. from αἴρω = redupl. + root + tense formative + 3ʳᵈ sg. ending (ἠ +ρ + κε + ν).

COLOSSIANS 2

ἐκ τοῦ μέσου προσηλώσας¹ αὐτὸ τῷ σταυρῷ².
15 ἀπεκδυσάμενος³ τὰς ἀρχὰς καὶ τὰς ἐξουσίας ἐδειγμάτισεν⁴ ἐν παρρησίᾳ,⁵ θριαμβεύσας⁶ αὐτοὺς ἐν αὐτῷ⁷.
16 Μὴ οὖν τις ὑμᾶς κρινέτω⁸ ἐν βρώσει⁹ ⌐ἢ¬¹⁰ ἐν πόσει¹¹ ἢ ἐν μέρει¹² ἑορτῆς¹³ ἢ νουμηνίας¹⁴ ἢ σαββάτων, 17 ἅ ἐστιν σκιὰ¹⁵ τῶν μελλόντων,¹⁶ τὸ δὲ σῶμα¹⁷ ⌐τοῦ Χριστοῦ. 18 μηδεὶς ὑμᾶς καταβραβευέτω¹⁸ θέλων ἐν ταπεινοφροσύνῃ¹⁹ καὶ θρησκείᾳ²⁰ τῶν ἀγγέλων, ⌐ἃ ἑόρακεν²¹ ἐμβατεύων²², εἰκῇ²³ φυσιούμενος²⁴ ὑπὸ τοῦ

---

1 προσηλόω, *I nail, fasten with nails, pin.*
2 σταυρός, ου, ὁ, *cross.*
3 ἀπεκδύομαι, *I remove, strip off, undress.*
4 δειγματίζω, *I disgrace, expose, make a show of.*
5 παρρησία, ας, ἡ, *boldness.*
6 θριαμβεύω, *I triumph over, lead in triumphal procession.*
7 TH: referent is τῷ σταυρῷ, *the cross.*
8 MH: pres. act. impv. 3rd sg.
9 βρῶσις, εως, ἡ, *food, eating.*
10 NA²⁸ indicates some MSS do not have ἤ.
11 πόσις, εως, ἡ, *drink, drinking.*
12 μέρος, ους, τό, *part.*
13 ἑορτή, ῆς, ἡ, *feast, festival.*
14 Contracted form of νεομηνία, ας, ἡ, *new moon, first of the month.* The NA²⁸ has νεομηνίας.
15 σκιά, ᾶς, ἡ, *shadow.*
16 TH: subst. prtc. from μέλλω, *of the coming things.*
17 TH: verbless clause, *but the body belongs to Christ.*
18 καταβραβεύω, *I decide against, disqualify.*
19 ταπεινοφροσύνη, ης, ἡ, *humility.*
20 θρησκεία, ας, ἡ, *religion, worship.*
21 MH: pf. act. ind. 3ʳᵈ sg ὁράω = redupl. + root + tense formative + 3ʳᵈ sg. ending (ἑ + ορα + κε + ν).
22 ἐμβατεύω, *I enter in.*
23 εἰκῇ, adv. *without cause, without reason.*
24 φυσιόω, *I puff up.* TH: metaph. *make arrogant.*

43

ΠΡΟΣ ΚΟΛΟΣΣΑΕΙΣ

νοός[1] τῆς σαρκός[2] αὐτοῦ, 19 καὶ οὐ κρατῶν[3] τὴν κεφαλήν, ἐξ οὗ πᾶν τὸ σῶμα διὰ τῶν ἁφῶν[4] καὶ συνδέσμων[5] ἐπιχορηγούμενον[6] καὶ συμβιβαζόμενον[7] αὔξει[8] τὴν αὔξησιν[9] τοῦ θεοῦ.

20 Εἰ ἀπεθάνετε σὺν Χριστῷ ἀπὸ τῶν στοιχείων[10] τοῦ κόσμου, τί[11] ὡς ζῶντες ἐν κόσμῳ δογματίζεσθε·[12] 21 Μὴ ἅψῃ[13] μηδὲ γεύσῃ[14] μηδὲ θίγῃς[15], 22 ἅ ἐστιν πάντα εἰς φθορὰν[16] τῇ ἀποχρήσει,[17] κατὰ τὰ ἐντάλματα[18] καὶ διδασκαλίας[19] τῶν ἀνθρώπων; 23 ἅτινά

---

1 νοῦς, νοός, ὁ, *mind, intellect.*
2 TH: τῆς σαρκός, attrib. gen., *fleshly mind.*
3 κρατέω, *I take hold of, grasp.*
4 ἁφή, ῆς, ἡ, *ligament.*
5 σύνδεσμος, ου, ὁ, *bond, link, sinew.*
6 ἐπιχορηγέω, *I furnish, supply.* MH: pres. pass. prtc. nom. neut. sg. TH: attrib. part. with τὸ σῶμα.
7 συμβιβάζω, *I unite, bring together.* MH: pres. pass. prtc. nom. neut. sg. TH: attrib. part. with τὸ σῶμα.
8 αὐξάνω, *I cause to grow, increase.*
9 αὔξησις, *growth, increase.* TH: cognate acc.
10 στοιχεῖον, ου, τό, *element, element of nature.* TH: occurs only in pl. in the NT, *elemental properties* or *principles.*
11 TH: τί begins question that ends in 2:22, *why....?*
12 δογματίζω, *I decree.* TH: only in mid./pass. in NT, *submit to rules.* Permissive pass. implies subjects' consent.
13 ἅπτω, *I light, ignite, kindle; I touch, handle* (mid.) ; MH: aor. mid. subj. 2nd sg. TH: prohibitive subj. functions as impv.
14 γεύομαι, *I taste.* MH: aor. mid. subj. 2nd sg. TH: prohibitive subj. functions as impv.
15 θιγγάνω, *I touch.* MH: aor. mid. subj. 2nd sg. TH: prohibitive subj. functions as impv.
16 φθορά, ᾶς, ἡ, *destruction, ruin, decay.*
17 ἀπόχρησις, εως, ἡ, *use, using up.* TH: dat. of means.
18 ἔνταλμα, τος, τό, *command, commandment.*
19 διδασκαλία, ας, ἡ, *teaching.*

COLOSSIANS 2

ἐστιν λόγον μὲν¹ ἔχοντα² σοφίας ἐν ἐθελοθρησκίᾳ³ καὶ ταπεινοφροσύνῃ⁴ καὶ ἀφειδίᾳ⁵ σώματος, οὐκ⁶ ἐν τιμῇ⁷ τινι πρὸς πλησμονὴν⁸ τῆς σαρκός.

---

1 TH: intensive, *indeed*.
2 TH: periph. prtc. with ἐστιν having λόγον...σοφίας as dir. obj., *which things are indeed having a word of wisdom*.
3 ἐθελοθρησκία, ας, ἡ, *self-made religion, self-made worship*. TH: *self-generated piety*.
4 ταπεινοφροσύνη, ης, ἡ, *humility*.
5 ἀφειδία, ας, ἡ, *harsh treatment*.
6 TH: begins an implied concessive statement, *(although) not with any value against (the) indulgence of the flesh*.
7 τιμή, ῆς, ἡ, *honor, price,* **value**.
8 πλησμονή, ῆς, ἡ, *fullness, satisfaction, indulgence*. TH: πρός may signify *against* and τῆς σαρκός may be an obj. gen., *against (the) indulgence of the flesh*.

ΠΡΟΣ ΚΟΛΟΣΣΑΕΙΣ

Colossians 3

New Vocabulary by Frequency in Chapter
[Occurrences in Book, Chapter, SBLGNT]

φανερόω, *I make known, reveal* [4, 2, 49]
ἐργάζομαι, *I work, perform* [1, 1, 41]
ἐπιθυμία, ας, ἡ, *desire, lust* [1, 1, 38]
εὐχαριστέω, *I thank; give thanks* [2, 1, 38]
ὑποτάσσω, *I am subject* [1, 1, 38]
ὀργή, ῆς, ἡ, *anger* [1, 1, 36]
περιτομή, ῆς, ἡ, *circumcision* [4, 1, 36]
μέλος, ους, τό, *member, limb* [1, 1, 34]
ποτέ, adv. *then* [1, 1, 29]
ἀδικέω, *I do wrong, harm* [2, 2, 28]
πνευματικός, η, ον, adj. *spiritual* [2, 1, 26]
δουλεύω, *I serve* [1, 1, 25]
Ἕλλην, ηνος, ὁ, *Greek* [1, 1, 25]
πορνεία, ας, ἡ, *fornication* [1, 1, 25]
εἰκών, όνος, ἡ, *image* [2, 1, 23]
ἐλεύθερος, α, ον, adj. *free* [1, 1, 23]
νέος, α, ον, adj. *new* [1, 1, 23]
χαρίζομαι, *I give freely, forgive* [2, 1, 23]
ἐκλεκτός, η, ον, adj. *chosen, elect* [1, 1, 22]
ὑπακούω, *I obey* [2, 2, 21]
ἀκροβυστία, ας, ἡ, *uncircumcision, foreskin* [2, 1, 20]
γονεύς, εως, ἡ, *parent* [1, 1, 20]
ἐπίγνωσις, εως, ἡ, *knowledge, full knowledge* [3, 1, 20]
νυνί, adv. *now, at this moment* [2, 1, 20]
παλαιός, α, ον, adj. *old* [1, 1, 19]
βλασφημία, ας, ἡ, *blasphemy* [1, 1, 18]
θυμός, ου, ὁ, *wrath, rage* [1, 1, 18]
κρύπτω, *I hide, conceal* [1, 1, 18]

COLOSSIANS 3

ἀνέχω, *I put up with, bear with, endure* [1, 1, 15]
κτίζω, *I create* [3, 1, 15]
κληρονομία, ας, ἡ, *inheritance* [1, 1, 14]
μακροθυμία, ας, ἡ, *longsuffering, forbearance* [2, 1, 14]
ψεύδομαι, *I lie* [1, 1, 12]
κακία, ας, ἡ, *evil, malice* [1, 1, 11]
πραΰτης, ητος, ἡ, *gentleness, meekness, courtesy* [1, 1, 11]
σπλάγχνον, ου, τό, *inward parts, intestines, viscera,* metaph. *heart* [1, 1, 11]
ἀκαθαρσία, ας, ἡ, *uncleanness* [1, 1, 10]
ἀπολαμβάνω, *I receive from* [1, 1, 10]
κομίζω, *I receive, receive back* [1, 1, 10]
πλεονεξία, ας, ἡ, *covetousness* [1, 1, 10]
χρηστότης, ητος, ἡ, *goodness, kindness* [1, 1, 10]
ἄνω, adj. *up, above* [2, 2, 9]
ἀποτίθημι, *I put off, get rid of, cease from* [1, 1, 9]
εὐάρεστος, ον, adj. *well-pleasing, acceptable* [1, 1, 9]
ἁπλότης, ητος, ἡ, *simplicity, sincerity, integrity* [1, 1, 8]
νουθετέω, *I admonish, exhort* [2, 1, 8]
ταπεινοφροσύνη, ης, ἡ, *humility* [2, 1, 7]
ψαλμός, ου, ὁ, *psalm* [1, 1, 7]
ᾠδή, ης, ἡ, *song, ode* [1, 1, 7]
βάρβαρος, ον, adj. *barbarian* [1, 1, 6]
πρᾶξις, εως, ἡ, *practice* [1, 1, 6]
ᾄδω, *I sing* [1, 1, 5]
ἐνοικέω, *I dwell in* [1, 1, 5]
οἰκτιρμός, οῦ, ὁ, *pity, compassion* [1, 1, 5]
ἀπείθεια, ας, ἡ, *disobedience* [1, 1, 4]
εἰδωλολατρία, ας, ἡ, *idolatry* [1, 1, 4]
ἔνειμι, *I am in, within, among* [1, 1, 4]
πικραίνω, *I make bitter, embitter, resentful* [1, 1, 4]
πλουσίως, adv. *richly, abundantly* [1, 1, 4]
προσωπολημψία, ας, ἡ, *partiality, favoritism* [1, 1, 4]
σύνδεσμος, ου, ὁ, *bond, link* [2, 1, 4]

47

ΠΡΟΣ ΚΟΛΟΣΣΑΕΙΣ

φρονέω, *I think* [1, 1, 4]
ἀνήκω, *I am fit, fitting, proper* [1, 1, 3]
νεκρόω, *I put to death, kill* [1, 1, 3]
πάθος, ους, τό, *passion, emotion, suffering* [1, 1, 3]
συνεγείρω, *I raise with, raise up with* [2, 1, 3]
ἀνακαινόω, *I renew* [1, 1, 2]
ἀνθρωπάρεσκος, ον, adj. *people pleaser* [1, 1, 2]
ἀπεκδύομαι, *I remove, strip off, undress* [2, 1, 2]
ἐρεθίζω, *I provoke* [1, 1, 2]
τελειότης, ητος, ἡ, *perfection, completeness, maturity* [1, 1, 2]
ὕμνος, ου, ὁ, *hymn, song of praise* [1, 1, 2]
ἀθυμέω, *I am discouraged, disheartened* [1, 1, 1]
αἰσχρολογία, ας, ἡ, *obscene speech* [1, 1, 1]
ἀνταπόδοσις, εως, ἡ, *reward, recompense, repay* [1, 1, 1]
βραβεύω, *I judge, rule* [1, 1, 1]
εὐχάριστος, ον, adj. *thankful* [1, 1, 1]
μομφή, ης, ἡ, *complaint* [1, 1, 1]
ὀφθαλμοδουλία, ας, ἡ, *eye service, service given without dedication* [1, 1, 1]
Σκύθης, ου, ὁ, *Scythian* [1, 1, 1]

ns 3

3:1 Εἰ οὖν συνηγέρθητε¹ τῷ Χριστῷ, τὰ ἄνω² ζητεῖτε, οὗ³ ὁ Χριστός ἐστιν ἐν δεξιᾷ τοῦ θεοῦ καθήμενος· 2 τὰ ἄνω⁴ φρονεῖτε⁵, μὴ τὰ ἐπὶ τῆς γῆς⁶, 3 ἀπεθάνετε γάρ, καὶ ἡ ζωὴ ὑμῶν κέκρυπται⁷ σὺν τῷ Χριστῷ ἐν τῷ θεῷ· 4 ὅταν ὁ Χριστὸς φανερωθῇ⁸, ἡ ζωὴ ⌐ὑμῶν⁹, τότε καὶ¹⁰ ὑμεῖς σὺν αὐτῷ φανερωθήσεσθε¹¹ ἐν δόξῃ.

5 Νεκρώσατε¹² οὖν τὰ ⌐μέλη¹³ τὰ ἐπὶ τῆς γῆς¹⁴, πορνείαν¹⁵, ἀκαθαρσίαν¹⁶, πάθος¹⁷, ἐπιθυμίαν¹⁸ κακήν, καὶ τὴν πλεονεξίαν¹⁹ ἥτις ἐστὶν εἰδωλολατρία²⁰, 6 δι' ἃ²¹ ἔρχεται ἡ ὀργὴ²² τοῦ θεοῦ ⌐ἐπὶ τοὺς υἱοὺς τῆς

---

1 συνεγείρω, *I raise with, raise up with*. TH: followed by dat. of association.
2 ἄνω, adv. *up, above*. TH: subst. adv., *the things above*.
3 ὅς, ἥ, ὅ, *who, which, that*. TH: gen. rel. pron. functions as adv. *where*.
4 ἄνω, adv. *up, above*. TH: subst. adv., *the things above*.
5 φρονέω, *I think*.
6 TH: subst. prep. phrase, *the things upon the earth*.
7 κρύπτω, *I hide, conceal*. MH: pf. mid. ind. 2ⁿᵈ pl.
8 φανερόω, *I make known, reveal*. MH: aor. pass. subj. 2ⁿᵈ pl.
9 NA²⁸ indicates some MSS read ἡμῶν.
10 TH: ascensive or additive καί, *also, even*.
11 φανερόω, *I make known, reveal*. MH: fut. pass. ind. 2ⁿᵈ pl.
12 νεκρόω, *I put to death, kill*.
13 μέλος, ους, τό, *member, limb*. TH: the *members* or *parts* of the body. NA²⁸ indicates some MSS read μέλη ὑμῶν.
14 TH: subst. prep. phrase, *the things upon the earth*.
15 πορνεία, ας, ἡ, *fornication*.
16 ἀκαθαρσία, ας, ἡ, *uncleanness*.
17 πάθος, ους, τό, *passion, emotion, suffering*
18 ἐπιθυμία, ας, ἡ, *desire, lust*.
19 πλεονεξία, ας, ἡ, *covetousness*.
20 εἰδωλολατρία, ας, ἡ, *idolatry*.
21 TH: δι' ἃ indicates cause, *on account of which things*.
22 ὀργή, ῆς, ἡ, *anger, wrath*.

ΠΡΟΣ ΚΟΛΟΣΣΑΕΙΣ

ἀπειθείας[1]· 7 ἐν οἷς καὶ[2] ὑμεῖς περιεπατήσατέ ποτε[3] ὅτε ἐζῆτε[4] ἐν ⌜τούτοις·[5] 8 νυνὶ[6] δὲ ἀπόθεσθε[7] καὶ[8] ὑμεῖς τὰ πάντα, ὀργήν[9], θυμόν[10], κακίαν[11], βλασφημίαν[12], αἰσχρολογίαν[13] ἐκ τοῦ στόματος ὑμῶν· 9 μὴ ψεύδεσθε[14] εἰς ἀλλήλους· ἀπεκδυσάμενοι[15] τὸν παλαιὸν[16] ἄνθρωπον σὺν ταῖς πράξεσιν[17] αὐτοῦ, 10 καὶ ἐνδυσάμενοι[18] τὸν νέον[19] τὸν ἀνακαινούμενον[20] εἰς ἐπίγνωσιν[21] κατ᾽

---

1 ἀπειθεία, ας, ἡ, *disobedience*. Some MSS omit ἐπὶ τοὺς υἱοὺς τῆς ἀπειθείας.
2 TH: ascensive or additive καί, *also, even*.
3 ποτέ, particle, *then, once, formerly*.
4 MH: impf. act. ind. 2nd pl. from ζάω, *you were living*.
5 NA²⁸ indicates some MSS read αὐτοῖς.
6 νυνί, adv. *now, at this moment*, emphatic form of νῦν strengthened by ι demonstrative.
7 ἀποτίθημι, *I put off, get rid of, cease from*. MH: aor. mid. impv. = prefix + root+ tense formative + impv. mid. ending (ἀπο + θε + σ + θε). Nonindicative, non-present tense -μι verbs drop redupl. of the first letter of the root word.
8 TH: ascensive or additive καί, *also, even*.
9 ὀργή, ῆς, ἡ, *anger*. TH: app. to τὰ πάντα.
10 θυμός, οῦ, ὁ, *wrath, rage*. TH: app. to τὰ πάντα.
11 κακία, ας, ἡ, *evil, malice*. TH: app. to τὰ πάντα.
12 βλασφημία, ας, ἡ, *blasphemy*. TH: app. to τὰ πάντα.
13 αἰσχρολογία, ας, ἡ, *obscene speech*. TH: app. to τὰ πάντα.
14 ψεύδομαι, *I lie*. TH: μή helps identify as impv.
15 ἀπεκδύομαι, *I remove, strip off, undress*. TH: adv. prtc. with ψεύδεσθε.
16 παλαιός, ά, όν, adj. *old*.
17 πρᾶξις, εως, ἡ, *practice, activity, action*.
18 ἐνδύω, *I put on, clothe*.
19 νέος, α, ον, adj. *new*. TH: subst. adj., *the new person*.
20 ἀνακαινόω, *I renew*. MH: pres. pass. prtc. acc. masc. sg.
21 ἐπίγνωσις, εως, ἡ, *knowledge, full knowledge*.

εἰκόνα¹ τοῦ κτίσαντος² αὐτόν, 11 ὅπου οὐκ ἔνι³ ⸂Ἕλλην⁴ καὶ Ἰουδαῖος, περιτομὴ⁵ καὶ ἀκροβυστία⁶, βάρβαρος⁷, Σκύθης⁸, δοῦλος, ἐλεύθερος⁹, ἀλλὰ ⸀τὰ πάντα¹⁰ καὶ ἐν πᾶσιν Χριστός.

12 Ἐνδύσασθε¹¹ οὖν ὡς ἐκλεκτοὶ¹² τοῦ θεοῦ, ἅγιοι¹³ καὶ ἠγαπημένοι¹⁴, σπλάγχνα¹⁵ οἰκτιρμοῦ¹⁶, χρηστότητα¹⁷, ταπεινοφροσύνην¹⁸, πραΰτητα¹⁹, μακροθυμίαν²⁰, 13 ἀνεχόμενοι²¹ ἀλλήλων καὶ χαριζόμενοι²² ἑαυτοῖς ἐάν τις πρός τινα ἔχῃ μομφήν²³·

1 εἰκών, όνος, ἡ, image.
2 κτίζω, I create. TH: subst. prtc., the one who created it.
3 ἔνειμι, I am in, within, among. TH: ἔνι = ἔνεστι(ν), pres. act. ind. 3ʳᵈ sg. of ἔνειμι.
4 Ἕλλην, ηνος, ὁ, Greek.
5 περιτομή, ῆς, ἡ, circumcision.
6 ἀκροβυστία, ας, ἡ, uncircumcision, foreskin.
7 βάρβαρος, ον, adj. barbarian.
8 Σκύθης, ου, ὁ, Scythian.
9 ἐλεύθερος, α, ον, adj. free.
10 TH: τὰ πάντα pred. nom. with Χριστός as subject, Christ is all things and in all. Some MSS do not have the article τά.
11 ἐνδύω, I put on, clothe.
12 ἐκλεκτός, ή, όν, adj. chosen, elect. TH: subst., chosen of God.
13 TH: subst. adj. in app. to ἐκλεκτοί.
14 MH: pf. pass. prtc. nom. masc. pl. TH: subst. prtc. app. to ἐκλεκτοί.
15 σπλάγχνον, ου, τό, inward parts, intestines, viscera, metaph. heart. TH: begins list of dir. objs. of Ἐνδύσασθε.
16 οἰκτιρμός, οῦ, ὁ, pity, compassion.
17 χρηστότης, ητος, ἡ, goodness, kindness.
18 ταπεινοφροσύνη, ης, ἡ, humility.
19 πραΰτης, ητος, ἡ, gentleness, meekness, courtesy.
20 μακροθυμία, ας, ἡ, longsuffering, forbearance. cmpd.
21 ἀνέχω, I put up with, bear with, endure (with gen.). TH: occurs only in mid. ἀνέχομαι in NT.
22 χαρίζομαι, I give freely, forgive (with dat.).
23 μομφή, ης, ἡ, complaint. NA²⁸ indicates some MSS read μέμψιν

ΠΡΟΣ ΚΟΛΟΣΣΑΕΙΣ

καθὼς καὶ[1] ὁ ⌜κύριος[2] ἐχαρίσατο[3] ὑμῖν οὕτως καὶ[4] ὑμεῖς[5]· 14 ἐπὶ πᾶσιν δὲ τούτοις τὴν ἀγάπην, ⌜ὅ[6] ἐστιν σύνδεσμος[7] τῆς τελειότητος[8]. 15 καὶ ἡ εἰρήνη τοῦ ⌜Χριστοῦ[9] βραβευέτω[10] ἐν ταῖς καρδίαις ὑμῶν, εἰς ἣν καὶ[11] ἐκλήθητε[12] ἐν ἑνὶ σώματι· καὶ εὐχάριστοι[13] γίνεσθε. 16 ὁ λόγος τοῦ Χριστοῦ ἐνοικείτω[14] ἐν ὑμῖν πλουσίως[15] ἐν πάσῃ σοφίᾳ· διδάσκοντες[16] καὶ νουθετοῦντες[17] ἑαυτοὺς ⌜ψαλμοῖς[18], ⌜ὕμνοις[19], ᾠδαῖς[20] πνευματικαῖς[21] ⌜ἐν χάριτι[22], ᾄδοντες[23] ἐν ⌜ταῖς καρδίαις[1⌝]

(μέμψις), *reason for complaint*.
1 TH: ascensive or additive καί, *also, even*.
2 NA²⁸ indicates some MSS read Χριστός.
3 χαρίζομαι, *I give freely, forgive* (with dat.).
4 TH: ascensive or additive καί, *also, even*.
5 TH: ὑμεῖς is nom. subject of implied χαρίζετε.
6 NA²⁸ indicates some MSS read ἥτις.
7 σύνδεσμος, ου, ὁ, *bond, link*. Cf 2:19, *sinew*. TH: pred. nom.
8 τελειότης, ητος, ἡ, *perfection, completeness, maturity*.
9 NA²⁸ indicates some MSS read θεοῦ.
10 βραβεύω, *I judge, rule*. MH: Pres. act. impv. 3rd sg.
11 TH: ascensive or additive καί, *also, even*.
12 MH: aor. pass. ind. 2ⁿᵈ pl.
13 εὐχάριστος, ον, adj. *thankful*. TH: pred. nom. of γίνεσθε.
14 ἐνοικέω, *I dwell in*. MH: pres. act. impv. 3ʳᵈ sg. TH: *let it dwell*.
15 πλουσίως, adv. *richly, abundantly*.
16 TH: nom. abs. with νουθετοῦντες and ᾄδοντες, although possibly with implied ἐσμέν (thus periphr. prtc.) or more likely elaborating how the Colossians participate in letting the Word of Christ dwell among themselves.
17 νουθετέω, *I admonish, exhort*.
18 ψαλμός, ου, ὁ, *psalm*.
19 ὕμνος, ου, ὁ, *hymn, song of praise*.
20 ᾠδή, ῆς, ἡ, *song, ode*.
21 πνευματικός, ή, όν, adj. *spiritual*.
22 NA²⁸ indicates some MSS read ἐν τῇ χάριτι.
23 ᾄδω, *I sing*.

ὑμῶν τῷ ⸂θεῷ⸃². 17 καὶ πᾶν ⸂ὅ τι⸃ ⸂ἐὰν ποιῆτε ἐν λόγῳ ἢ ἐν ἔργῳ, πάντα³ ἐν ὀνόματι κυρίου Ἰησοῦ⁴, εὐχαριστοῦντες⁵ τῷ ⸂θεῷ πατρὶ⁶ δι᾽ αὐτοῦ.

18 Αἱ γυναῖκες⁷, ὑποτάσσεσθε⁸ ⸂τοῖς ἀνδράσιν⁹, ὡς ἀνῆκεν¹⁰ ἐν κυρίῳ. 19 οἱ ἄνδρες¹¹, ἀγαπᾶτε τὰς γυναῖκας¹² καὶ μὴ πικραίνεσθε¹³ πρὸς αὐτάς.

20 Τὰ τέκνα¹⁴, ὑπακούετε¹⁵ τοῖς γονεῦσιν¹⁶ κατὰ πάντα, τοῦτο γὰρ ⸂εὐάρεστόν¹⁷ ἐστιν⸃ ἐν κυρίῳ. 21 οἱ πατέρες¹⁸, μὴ ἐρεθίζετε¹⁹ τὰ τέκνα ὑμῶν, ἵνα μὴ ἀθυμῶσιν²⁰. 22 οἱ δοῦλοι²¹, ὑπακούετε²² κατὰ πάντα τοῖς κατὰ σάρκα κυρίοις²³, μὴ ἐν ⸂ὀφθαλμοδουλίαις¹, ὡς

---

1 NA²⁸ indicates some MSS read τῇ καρδίᾳ.
2 NA²⁸ indicates some MSS read κυρίῳ.
3 TH: dir. obj. of an implied impv. verb ποιεῖτε.
4 NA²⁸ indicates some MSS read Ἰησοῦ Χριστοῦ.
5 εὐχαριστέω, I thank, give thanks.
6 TH: πατρὶ app. to θεῷ. NA²⁸ indicates some MSS read θεῷ καὶ πατρὶ.
7 MH: voc.
8 ὑποτάσσω, I subject. TH: pres. mid. impv. 2nd pl.
9 NA²⁸ indicates some MSS read ἀνδράσιν ὑμῶν or ἰδίοις ἀνδράσιν.
10 ἀνήκω, I am fit, fitting, proper.
11 MH: voc.
12 NA²⁸ indicates some MSS read γυναῖκας ὑμῶν.
13 πικραίνω, I make bitter, embitter, resentful. MH: pres. pass. impv. 2ⁿᵈ pl.
14 MH: voc.
15 ὑπακούω, I obey (with dat.).
16 γονεύς, εως, ἡ, parent.
17 εὐάρεστος, ον, adj. well-pleasing, acceptable.
18 MH: voc.
19 ἐρεθίζω, I provoke.
20 ἀθυμέω, I am discouraged, disheartened. MH: pres. act. subj. 3ʳᵈ pl.
21 MH: voc.
22 ὑπακούω, I obey (with dat.).
23 TH: masters (=slave masters).

ΠΡΟΣ ΚΟΛΟΣΣΑΕΙΣ

ἀνθρωπάρεσκοι², ἀλλ' ἐν ἁπλότητι³ καρδίας, φοβούμενοι τὸν ⌜κύριον⁴. 23 ⌜ὃ ἐὰν⁵ ποιῆτε, ἐκ ψυχῆς⁶ ἐργάζεσθε⁷, ὡς τῷ κυρίῳ καὶ οὐκ ἀνθρώποις, 24 εἰδότες⁸ ὅτι ἀπὸ κυρίου ⌜ἀπολήμψεσθε⁹ τὴν ἀνταπόδοσιν¹⁰ τῆς κληρονομίας¹¹· ⌜τῷ κυρίῳ Χριστῷ δουλεύετε¹²· 25 ὁ ⌜γὰρ ἀδικῶν¹³ κομίσεται¹⁴ ὃ ἠδίκησεν¹⁵, καὶ οὐκ ἔστιν προσωπολημψία¹⁶.

---

1 ὀφθαλμοδουλία, ας, ἡ, *eye service, service given without dedication*. NA²⁸ here reads ὀφθαλμοδουλίᾳ.
2 ἀνθρωπάρεσκος, ον, adj. *people pleaser*. TH: subst. adj.
3 ἁπλότης, ητος, ἡ, *simplicity, sincerity, integrity*. TH: with attibuted gen., *with sincerity of heart*.
4 NA²⁸ indicates some MSS read θεόν.
5 TH: ὃ ἐάν, *whatever*. NA²⁸ indicates some MSS read ὃ καὶ πᾶν.
6 TH: idiomatically *strongly, devotedly, energetically*.
7 ἐργάζομαι, *I work, perform*.
8 MH: pf. prtc. nom. masc. pl.
9 ἀπολαμβάνω, *I receive from*. NA²⁸ indicates some MSS read λήμψεσθε.
10 ἀνταπόδοσις, εως, ἡ, *reward, recompense, repay*.
11 κληρονομία, ας, ἡ, *inheritance*. TH: app. gen. to ἀνταπόδοσιν.
12 δουλεύω, *I serve* (with dat.).
13 ἀδικέω, *I do wrong, harm*.
14 κομίζω, *I receive, receive back*.
15 ἀδικέω, *I do wrong, harm*.
16 προσωπολημψία, ας, ἡ, *partiality, favoritism*. TH: and *there is no partiality*.

Colossians 4

New Vocabulary by Frequency in Chapter
[Occurrences in Book, Chapter, SBLGNT]

παραλαμβάνω, *I receive, take* [2, 1, 49]
φανερόω, *I make known, reveal* [4, 1, 49]
πάντοτε, adv. *always, at all times* [3, 2, 41]
θύρα, ας, ἡ, *door* [1, 1, 39]
περιτομή, ῆς, ἡ, *circumcision* [4, 1, 36]
προσευχή, ῆς, ἡ, *prayer* [2, 2, 36]
διακονία, ας, ἡ, *service* [1, 1, 34]
ἀναγινώσκω, *I read* [3, 3, 32]
διάκονος, ου, ὁ, *servant* [4, 1, 29]
Βαρναβᾶς, α, ὁ, *Barnabas* [1, 1, 28]
μυστήριον, ου, τό, *mystery* [4, 1, 28]
γνωρίζω, *I make known, reveal* [3, 2, 25]
ἐπιστολή, ῆς, ἡ, *letter* [1, 1, 24]
γρηγορέω, *I watch, am watchful, awake, alert* [1, 1, 22]
δέομαι, *I bind, imprison* [1, 1, 22]
μνημονεύω, *I remember* [1, 1, 21]
τέλειος, α, ον, *perfect, complete, mature* [2, 1, 19]
δεσμός, ου, ὁ, *bond, chain, imprisonment* [1, 1, 18]
εὐχαριστία, ας, ἡ, *thanksgiving* [2, 1, 15]
συνεργός, ου, ὁ, *fellow-worker, co-worker* [1, 1, 13]
ἅμα, adv. *at the same time* [1, 1, 10]
ἀσπασμός, ου, ὁ, *greeting* [1, 1, 10]
προσκαρτερέω, *I continue in, adhere to* [1, 1, 10]
σύνδουλος, ου, ὁ, *fellow slave* [2, 1, 10]
ἀγωνίζομαι, *I contend for a prize, fight, struggle* [2, 1, 8]
ἅλας, ατος, τό, *salt* [1, 1, 8]
Μᾶρκος, ου, ὁ, *Mark* [1, 1, 8]
ἰατρός, ου, ὁ, *physician* [1, 1, 7]

ΠΡΟΣ ΚΟΛΟΣΣΑΕΙΣ

Λαοδίκεια, ας, ἡ, Laodicea [4, 3, 6]
πληροφορέω, I fulfill, accomplish fully [1, 1, 6]
Ἀρίσταρχος, ου, ὁ, Aristarchus [1, 1, 5]
Τυχικός, ου, ὁ, Tychicus [1, 1, 5]
ἐξαγοράζω, I make the most of [1, 1, 4]
πόνος, ου, ὁ, labor, toil [1, 1, 4]
ἀρτύω, I season [1, 1, 3]
Δημᾶς, ᾶ, ὁ, Demas [1, 1, 3]
Ἐπαφρᾶς, ᾶ, ὁ, Epaphras [2, 1, 3]
Ἰοῦστος, ου, ὁ, Justus [1, 1, 3]
ἰσότης, ητος, ἡ, equality, fairness [1, 1, 3]
Λουκᾶς, ᾶ, ὁ, Luke [1, 1, 3]
συναιχμάλωτος, ου, ὁ, fellow-prisoner, fellow captive (of war. lit. taken with a spear) [1, 1, 3]
Ἀρχίππος, ου, ὁ, Archippus [1, 1, 2]
Ὀνήσιμος, ου, ὁ, Onesimus [1, 1, 2]
ἀνεψίος, ου, ὁ, cousin [1, 1, 1]
Ἱεράπολις, εως, ἡ, Hierapolis [1, 1, 1]
Νύμφα, ας, ἡ, Nympha [1, 1, 1]
παρηγορία, ας, ἡ, comfort [1, 1, 1]

COLOSSIANS 4

4:1 οἱ κύριοι¹, τὸ δίκαιον καὶ τὴν ἰσότητα² τοῖς δούλοις παρέχεσθε³, εἰδότες⁴ ὅτι καὶ⁵ ὑμεῖς ἔχετε κύριον ἐν ⌜οὐρανῷ⁶.

2 Τῇ προσευχῇ⁷ προσκαρτερεῖτε⁸, γρηγοροῦντες⁹ ἐν αὐτῇ¹⁰ ἐν εὐχαριστίᾳ¹¹, 3 προσευχόμενοι ἅμα¹² καὶ¹³ περὶ ἡμῶν, ἵνα ὁ θεὸς ἀνοίξῃ¹⁴ ἡμῖν θύραν¹⁵ τοῦ λόγου¹⁶, λαλῆσαι¹⁷ τὸ μυστήριον¹⁸ τοῦ Χριστοῦ, δι᾽ ὃ καὶ¹⁹ δέδεμαι²⁰, 4 ἵνα φανερώσω²¹ αὐτὸ ὡς δεῖ με²² λαλῆσαι. 5 Ἐν σοφίᾳ περιπατεῖτε πρὸς τοὺς ἔξω²³, τὸν καιρὸν

---

1 TH: *masters* (=*slave masters*). MH: voc.
2 ἰσότης, ητος, ἡ, *equality, fairness*.
3 παρέχω, *I offer, present*.
4 MH: pf. prtc. nom. masc. pl.
5 TH: ascensive or additive καί, *also, even*.
6 NA²⁸ indicates some MSS read οὐρανοῖς.
7 προσευχή, ῆς, ἡ, *prayer*.
8 προσκαρτερέω, *I continue in, adhere to* (with dat.). TH: impv.
9 γρηγορέω, *I watch, am watchful, awake, alert*.
10 TH: referent is Τῇ προσευχῇ.
11 εὐχαριστία, ας, ἡ, *thanksgiving*.
12 ἅμα, adv. *at the same time*.
13 TH: ascensive or additive καί, *also, even*.
14 MH: aor. act. subj. 3ʳᵈ sg.
15 θύρα, ας, ἡ, *door*.
16 TH: obj. gen., *a door for the word*.
17 TH: inf. of purpose.
18 μυστήριον, ου, τό, *mystery*.
19 TH: ascensive or additive καί, *also, even*.
20 δέω, *I bind, imprison*. MH: pf. pass. ind. 1ˢᵗ sg.
21 φανερόω, *I make known, reveal*. MH: aor. act. subj. 1ˢᵗ sg.
22 TH: acc. subject of inf. λαλῆσαι.
23 TH: subst. adv., *those outside*.

ΠΡΟΣ ΚΟΛΟΣΣΑΕΙΣ

ἐξαγοραζόμενοι[1]. 6 ὁ λόγος[2] ὑμῶν πάντοτε[3] ἐν χάριτι, ἅλατι[4] ἠρτυμένος[5], εἰδέναι[6] πῶς[7] δεῖ ὑμᾶς ἑνὶ ἑκάστῳ ἀποκρίνεσθαι.

7 Τὰ κατ' ἐμὲ πάντα[8] γνωρίσει[9] ὑμῖν Τυχικὸς[10] ὁ ἀγαπητὸς ἀδελφὸς καὶ πιστὸς διάκονος[11] καὶ σύνδουλος[12] ἐν κυρίῳ, 8 ὃν ἔπεμψα[13] πρὸς ὑμᾶς εἰς αὐτὸ[14] τοῦτο ἵνα ⌜γνῶτε[15] τὰ περὶ ⌜ἡμῶν[16] καὶ παρακαλέσῃ[17] τὰς καρδίας ὑμῶν, 9 σὺν Ὀνησίμῳ[18] τῷ πιστῷ καὶ ἀγαπητῷ ἀδελφῷ[19], ὅς ἐστιν ἐξ ὑμῶν· πάντα ὑμῖν γνωρίσουσιν[20] τὰ ὧδε[21].

---

1 ἐξαγοράζω, *I buy up, redeem, make the most of.* MH: pres. mid. prtc. nom. masc. pl.
2 TH: ὁ λόγος is subject of the implied impv., *let your speech be....*
3 πάντοτε, adv. *always, at all times.*
4 ἅλας, ατος, τό, *salt*
5 ἀρτύω, *I season.* MH: pf. pass. prtc. nom. masc. pl. = redupl. + root + pass. morpheme + nom. masc. ending (ἡ + ρτυ + μένο + ς).
6 MH: pf. act. inf. of οἶδα. TH: inf. of purpose.
7 TH: begins indir. question, *how it is necessary for you to respond to each one.*
8 TH: *all the things related to me.*
9 γνωρίζω, *I make known, reveal.*
10 Τυχικός, οῦ, ὁ, *Tychicus.*
11 διάκονος, ου, ὁ, *servant.* TH: ὁ ἀγαπητὸς ἀδελφὸς καὶ πιστὸς διάκονος καὶ σύνδουλος app. to Τυχικός. The article ὁ applies to all these app. nom. descriptors (Sharp's Rule).
12 σύνδουλος, ου, ὁ, *fellow slave.*
13 TH: epistolary aor., *I have sent.*
14 TH: intensive use of αὐτός, *the very thing.*
15 MH: aor. act. subj. 2nd pl.
16 NA^{28} indicates variant reading γνῷ τὰ περὶ ὑμῶν.
17 MH: aor. act. subj. 3rd sg.
18 Ὀνήσιμος, ου, ὁ, *Onesimus.*
19 TH: app. to Ὀνησίμῳ.
20 γνωρίζω, *I make known, reveal.*
21 TH: subst. adv., *the things here.*

10 Ἀσπάζεται ὑμᾶς Ἀρίσταρχος¹ ὁ συναιχμάλωτός² μου, καὶ Μᾶρκος³ ὁ ἀνεψιὸς⁴ Βαρναβᾶ⁵ (περὶ οὗ ἐλάβετε ἐντολάς, ἐὰν ἔλθῃ πρὸς ὑμᾶς δέξασθε αὐτόν), 11 καὶ Ἰησοῦς ὁ λεγόμενος⁶ Ἰοῦστος⁷, οἱ ὄντες ἐκ περιτομῆς⁸, οὗτοι μόνοι συνεργοὶ⁹ εἰς τὴν βασιλείαν τοῦ θεοῦ, οἵτινες ἐγενήθησάν μοι παρηγορία¹⁰. 12 ἀσπάζεται ὑμᾶς Ἐπαφρᾶς¹¹ ὁ ἐξ ὑμῶν¹², δοῦλος ⌐Χριστοῦ¹³, πάντοτε¹⁴ ἀγωνιζόμενος¹⁵ ὑπὲρ ὑμῶν ἐν ταῖς προσευχαῖς¹⁶, ἵνα ⌐σταθῆτε¹⁷ τέλειοι¹⁸ καὶ ⌐πεπληροφορημένοι¹⁹ ἐν παντὶ θελήματι τοῦ θεοῦ. 13 μαρτυρῶ

---

1 Ἀρίσταρχος, ου, ὁ, Aristarchus.
2 συναιχμάλωτος, ου, ὁ, fellow-prisoner, fellow captive (of war. lit. taken with a spear). TH: app. to Ἀρίσταρχος.
3 Μᾶρκος, ου, ὁ, Mark.
4 ἀνεψιός, ου, ὁ, cousin. TH: in app. to Μᾶρκος.
5 Βαρναβᾶς, ᾶ, ὁ, Barnabas. TH: gen. of rel.
6 MH: pres. pass. prtc. nom. masc. sg. TH: app. to Ἰησοῦς.
7 Ἰοῦστος, ου, ὁ, Justus.
8 περιτομή, ῆς, ἡ, circumcision. TH: descriptor in an app. statement, the ones from the circumcision.
9 συνεργός, οῦ, ὁ, fellow-worker, co-worker. TH: app. to οἱ ὄντες.
10 παρηγορία, ας, ἡ, comfort. TH: pred. nom.
11 Ἐπαφρᾶς, ᾶ, ὁ, Epaphras.
12 TH: attrib. position, the one from you.
13 TH: δοῦλος Χριστοῦ is app. to Ἐπαφρᾶς. NA²⁸ indicates some MSS read Χριστοῦ Ἰησοῦ.
14 πάντοτε, adv. always, at all times.
15 ἀγωνίζομαι, I struggle.
16 προσευχή, ῆς, ἡ, prayer.
17 MH: aor. pass. subj. 2ⁿᵈ pl. ἵστημι = root + aor. pass. tense formative + 2ⁿᵈ pl. ending (στα + θη + τε). Nonindicative, non-present tense - μι verbs drop redupl. of the first letter of the root word.
18 τέλειος, α, ον, perfect, complete, mature. TH: the nom. is retained obj. in agreement with the nom. subject with this passive verb, in order that you would stand mature.
19 πληροφορέω, I fulfill, accomplish fully. MH: pf. pass. prtc. nom.

ΠΡΟΣ ΚΟΛΟΣΣΑΕΙΣ

γὰρ αὐτῷ ὅτι ἔχει 'πολὺν πόνον¹⁾ ὑπὲρ ὑμῶν καὶ τῶν ἐν Λαοδικείᾳ² καὶ τῶν ἐν Ἱεραπόλει³. 14 ἀσπάζεται ὑμᾶς Λουκᾶς⁴ ὁ ἰατρὸς⁵ ὁ ἀγαπητὸς καὶ Δημᾶς⁶. 15 ἀσπάσασθε τοὺς ἐν Λαοδικείᾳ⁷ ἀδελφοὺς καὶ ⸀Νύμφαν⁸ καὶ τὴν κατ' οἶκον αὐτῆς⁹⁾ ἐκκλησίαν. 16 καὶ ὅταν ἀναγνωσθῇ¹⁰ παρ' ὑμῖν ἡ ἐπιστολή¹¹, ποιήσατε ἵνα καὶ¹² ἐν τῇ ⸀Λαοδικέων¹³ ἐκκλησίᾳ ἀναγνωσθῇ¹⁴, καὶ τὴν ἐκ Λαοδικείας¹⁵ ἵνα καὶ¹⁶ ὑμεῖς ἀναγνῶτε¹⁷. 17 καὶ εἴπατε¹⁸

---

    masc. pl. TH: see previous note.
1 πόνος, ου, ὁ, *labor, toil*.
2 Λαοδίκεια, ας, ἡ, *Laodicea*. TH: subst. prep. phrase, *those in Laodicea*.
3 Ἱεράπολις, εως, ἡ, *Hierapolis*. TH: subst. prep. phrase, *those in Hierapolis*.
4 Λουκᾶς, ᾶ, ὁ, *Luke*.
5 ἰατρός, ου, ὁ, *physician*. TH: in app. to Λουκᾶς, *the beloved physician*.
6 Δημᾶς, ᾶ, ὁ, *Demas*.
7 Λαοδίκεια, ας, ἡ, *Laodicea*.
8 Νύμφα, ας, ἡ, *Nympha*. This name could be masc. Νυμφᾶς or fem. Νύμφα.
9 NA²⁸ indicates the variants αὐτῶν and αὐτοῦ.
10 ἀναγινώσκω, *I read*. MH: aor. pass. subj. 3ʳᵈ sg. TH: indefinite temporal clause, *when(ever) it is read*.
11 ἐπιστολή, ῆς, ἡ, *letter*. TH: deictic art. with demonstrative force, *this letter*.
12 TH: ascensive or additive καί, *also, even*.
13 Λαοδίκεια, ας, ἡ, *Laodicea*.
14 ἀναγινώσκω, *I read*. MH: aor. pass. subj. 3ʳᵈ sg.
15 Λαοδίκεια, ας, ἡ, *Laodicea*. TH: τὴν implies ἐπιστολήν; this phrase is placed front of its clause that is initiated with ἵνα.
16 TH: ascensive or additive καί, *also, even*.
17 ἀναγινώσκω, *I read*. MH: aor. pass. subj. 2ⁿᵈ pl.
18 λέγω, *I say, speak*. MH: aor. act. impv.

COLOSSIANS 4

Ἀρχίππῳ¹· Βλέπε τὴν διακονίαν² ἣν παρέλαβες³ ἐν κυρίῳ, ἵνα αὐτὴν πληροῖς⁴. 18 Ὁ ἀσπασμὸς⁵ τῇ ἐμῇ χειρὶ Παύλου. μνημονεύετέ⁶ μου τῶν δεσμῶν⁷. ἡ χάρις μεθ᾽ ⌜ὑμῶν⁸.

---

1 Ἄρχιππος, ου, ὁ, Archippus.
2 διακονία, ας, ἡ, service.
3 παραλαμβάνω, I receive, take.
4 MH: aor. act. subj. 2nd sg.
5 ἀσπασμός, οῦ, ὁ, greeting. TH: subject of an implied verb ἐστίν.
6 μνημονεύω, I remember.
7 δεσμός, οῦ, ὁ, bond, chain, imprisonment.
8 TH: implied verb be with you. NA²⁸ indicates some MSS read ἡμῶν. Some close the letter with Ἀμήν.

Philemon

ΠΡΟΣ ΦΙΛΗΜΟΝΑ

ΠΡΟΣ ΦΙΛΗΜΟΝΑ

Philemon

New Vocabulary by Frequency in GNT and Alphabetized
[Occurrences in Book, SBLGNT]

οὐκέτι, adv. *no longer* [1,47]
σεαυτοῦ, ῆς, reflex. pron. *yourself* [1,43]
πάντοτε, adv. *always, at all times.* [1,41]
χωρίς, prep. *apart from* [1, 41]
ἑτοιμάζω, *I prepare, make or get ready, provide* [1,40]
εὐχαριστέω, *I thank, give thanks* [1,38]
βούλομαι, *I wish, want, desire* [1,37]
ἐμαυτοῦ, ῆς, reflex. pron. *myself* [1,37]
διακονέω, *I serve* [1,37]
προσευχή, ῆς, ἡ, *prayer* [2,36]
ὀφείλω, *I owe, am indebted, ought, am obligated* [1,35]
ναί, *yes* [1,33]
ἐλπίζω, *I hope, hope for, expect* [1,31]
παρρησία, ας, ἡ, *boldness, confidence* [1,31]
παράκλησις, εως, ἡ, *exhortation, comfort, encouragement* [1,29]
ποτέ, adv. *then* [1,29]
ἀδικέω, *I wrong, do wrong, injure* [1,28]
πόσος, η, ον, *how much, how many* [1,27]
ἀδελφή, ῆς, ἡ, *sister* [1,26]
σός, σή, σόν, adj. *your* [1,24]
Τιμόθεος, ου, ὁ, *Timothy* [1,24]
χαρίζομαι, *I give, grant, return* [1,23]
ἐπίγνωσις, εως, ἡ, *knowledge, full knowledge* [1,20]
νυνί, adv. *now, at this moment* [2,20]
ἀπέχω, *I have back* [1,19]
κοινωνία, ας, ἡ, *fellowship, association, sharing* [1,19]
δεσμός, ου, ὁ, *bond, chain, imprisonment* [2,18]
ἀνάγκη, ης, ἡ, *necessity, compulsion* [1,17]
κατέχω, *I keep, hold on to, hold back, restrain* [1,17]
δέσμιος, ου, ὁ, *prisoner, captive* [2,16]
ὑπακοή, ῆς, ἡ, *obedience* [1,15]
συνεργός, ου, ὁ, *fellow-worker, co-worker* [2,13]
χωρίζω, *I separate, depart, leave* [1,13]

PHILEMON

ἀναπαύω, *I cause to rest, refresh* [2,12]
μάλιστα, adv. *especially* [1,12]
προσλαμβάνω, *I welcome* [1,12]
σπλάγχνον, ου, τό, *inward parts, intestines, viscera,* metaph. *heart* [3,11]
ἅμα, adj, adv. *at the same time, together* [1,10]
ἐπιτάσσω, *I command* [1,10]
κοινωνός, ου, ὁ, *partner* [1,10]
γνώμη, ης, ἡ, *mind, purpose, consent* [1,9]
Μᾶρκος, ου, ὁ, *Mark* [1,8]
μνεία, ας, ἡ, *remembrance, memory, mention* [1,7]
ἀναπέμπω, *I send back* [1,5]
Ἀρίσταρχος, ου, ὁ, *Aristarchus* [1,5]
ἀνήκω, *I am fit, appropriate, proper* [1,3]
Δημᾶς, ᾶ, ὁ, *Demas* [1,3]
ἐνεργής, ές, *effective, active, powerful* [1,3]
Ἐπαφρᾶς, ᾶ, ὁ, *Epaphras* [1,3]
εὔχρηστος, ον, adj. *useful* [1,3]
Λουκᾶς, ᾶ, ὁ, *Luke* [1,3]
πρεσβύτης, ου, ὁ, *elder, old man* [1,3]
συναιχμάλωτος, ου, ὁ, *fellow-prisoner, fellow captive* [1,3]
Ἄρχιππος, ου, ὁ, *Archippus* [1,2]
ἐλλογέω, *I charge to one's account* [1,2]
ξενία, ας, ἡ, *hospitality, guest room* [1,2]
Ὀνήσιμος, ου, ὁ, *Onesimus* [1,2]
συστρατιώτης, ου, ὁ, *fellow-soldier* [1,2]
τάχα, adv. *perhaps, possibly* [1,2]
ἀποτίνω, *I repay* [1,1]
Ἀπφία, ας, ἡ, *Apphia* [1,1]
ἄχρηστος, ον, adj. *useless, worthless* [1,1]
ἑκούσιος, α, ον, adj. *voluntary* [1,1]
ὀνίνημι, *I benefit* [1,1]
προσοφείλω, *I owe, owe besides* [1,1]
Φιλήμων, ονος, ὁ, *Philemon* [1,1]

ΠΡΟΣ ΦΙΛΗΜΟΝΑ

1 Παῦλος[1] δέσμιος[2] Χριστοῦ Ἰησοῦ καὶ Τιμόθεος[3] ὁ ἀδελφὸς[4] Φιλήμονι[5] τῷ ἀγαπητῷ καὶ συνεργῷ[6] ἡμῶν 2 καὶ Ἀπφίᾳ[7] τῇ ⌜ἀδελφῇ[8] καὶ Ἀρχίππῳ[9] τῷ συστρατιώτῃ[10] ἡμῶν καὶ τῇ κατ' οἶκόν σου ἐκκλησίᾳ·[11] 3 χάρις ὑμῖν καὶ εἰρήνη ἀπὸ θεοῦ πατρὸς ἡμῶν καὶ κυρίου Ἰησοῦ Χριστοῦ.

4 Εὐχαριστῶ[12] τῷ θεῷ μου πάντοτε[13] μνείαν[14] σου ποιούμενος[15] ἐπὶ τῶν προσευχῶν[16] μου, 5 ἀκούων[17] σου

---

1 TH: nom. abs.
2 δέσμιος, ου, ὁ, *prisoner, captive*. TH: app. to Παῦλος, designates Paul as *a prisoner*.
3 Τιμόθεος, ου, ὁ, *Timothy*.
4 Παῦλος...ἀδελφὸς, TH: nom. abs. ὁ ἀδελφὸς app. to Τιμόθεος.
5 Φιλήμων, ονος, ὁ, *Philemon*.TH: dat. of recipient.
6 συνεργός, ου, ὁ, *fellow-worker, co-worker*.
7 Ἀπφία, ας, ἡ, *Apphia*. TH: dat. of recipient.
8 ἀδελφή, ῆς, ἡ, *sister*. NA²⁸ indicates some MSS read ἀδελφῇ ἀγαπητῇ.
9 Ἄρχιππος, ου, ὁ, *Archippus*. TH: dat. of recipient.
10 συστρατιώτης, ου, ὁ, *fellow-soldier*. TH: app. to Ἀρχίππῳ.
11 τῇ κατ' οἶκόν σου ἐκκλησίᾳ, TH: dat. of recipient. κατά with acc. here indicates place, location, *to the church in your house*.
12 εὐχαριστέω, *I thank; give thanks*.
13 πάντοτε, adv. *always, at all times*.
14 μνεία, ας, ἡ, *remembrance, memory, mention*. TH: *making mention of you*, idiomatically *remembering you*.
15 MH: pres. mid./pass. prtc. nom. masc. sg. of ποιέω = root + connecting vowel + mid./pass. prtc. morpheme + case ending (ποιε + ου + μενο + ς).
16 προσευχή, ῆς, ἡ, *prayer*. MH: gen. fem. pl.
17 MH: pres. act. nom. prtc. sg. of ἀκούω = root + connecting vowel + pres. prtc. morpheme (ἀκου + ο + ν), ο lengthens to ω, no case ending. TH: *hearing*.

PHILEMON

τὴν ἀγάπην καὶ τὴν πίστιν ἣν ἔχεις ⌜πρὸς¹ τὸν κύριον Ἰησοῦν καὶ εἰς πάντας τοὺς ἁγίους, 6 ὅπως ἡ κοινωνία² τῆς πίστεώς σου ἐνεργὴς³ γένηται⁴ ἐν ἐπιγνώσει⁵ παντὸς ἀγαθοῦ ⌜τοῦ⁶ ἐν ἡμῖν εἰς ⌜Χριστόν⁷. 7 ⌜χαρὰν γὰρ ⌜πολλὴν ἔσχον⁸⌝ καὶ παράκλησιν⁹ ἐπὶ τῇ ἀγάπῃ σου, ὅτι τὰ σπλάγχνα¹⁰ τῶν ἁγίων ἀναπέπαυται¹¹ διὰ σοῦ, ἀδελφέ¹².1
8 Διό,¹³ πολλὴν ἐν Χριστῷ παρρησίαν¹⁴ ἔχων ἐπιτάσσειν¹⁵ σοι τὸ ἀνῆκον¹⁶, 9 διὰ τὴν ἀγάπην μᾶλλον

---

1 NA²⁸ indicates some MSS read εἰς.
2 κοινωνία, ας, ἡ, *fellowship, association, sharing*.
3 ἐνεργής, ές, *effective, active, powerful*. TH: pred. adj. of γένηται, *would be effective*.
4 TH: ὅπως...γένηται, *so that the fellowship of your faith would become effective*.
5 ἐπίγνωσις, εως, ἡ, *knowledge, full knowledge*.
6 TH: παντὸς ἀγαθοῦ τοῦ is a subst. adj. with art. marking attrib. position, *every good thing (which is)*....
7 TH: ἐν ἐπιγνώσει...Χριστόν, *in (the) knowledge of every good thing in us for Christ*.
8 MH: 2nd aor. stem of ἔχω = ἐ (augment) + σεχ (root) > σχ (ε drops out; known as syncope) + ον (1st sg. ending).
9 παράκλησις, εως, ἡ, *exhortation, comfort, encouragement*.
10 σπλάγχνον, ου, τό, *inward parts, intestines, viscera*, metaph. **heart**.
11 ἀναπαύω, *I cause to rest*, **refresh**. MH: cmpd. ἀναπέπαυται = prep. + redupl. + root + pass. ending (ἀνα + πε + παυ + ται).
12 TH: voc. *brother*.
13 TH: inferential conj. developing the description of Philemon.
14 παρρησία, ας, ἡ, *boldness, confidence*. MH: d.o. of ἔχων and modified by πολλήν, *having much boldness*.
15 ἐπιτάσσω, *I command*. MH: pres. act. inf. TH: inf. of purpose with σοι τὸ ἀνῆκον as dir. objs., *to command you (to do) what is proper*.
16 ἀνήκω, *I am fit, appropriate, proper*. MH: pres. act. acc. prtc. neut. cmpd. ἀνῆκον = prep. + root + connecting vowel + pres. ptcp. neut. morpheme (ἀν + ηκ + ο + ον). TH: *what is proper*, i.e. what is the right thing.

ΠΡΟΣ ΦΙΛΗΜΟΝΑ

παρακαλῶ, τοιοῦτος ὢν ὡς¹ Παῦλος πρεσβύτης² νυνὶ³ δὲ καὶ⁴ δέσμιος⁵ Χριστοῦ Ἰησοῦ⟩— 10 παρακαλῶ σε περὶ τοῦ ἐμοῦ τέκνου, ὃν ἐγέννησα ἐν τοῖς ⌜δεσμοῖς⁶ Ὀνήσιμον,⁷ 11 τόν ποτέ⁸ σοι ἄχρηστον⁹ νυνὶ¹⁰ ⌜δὲ σοὶ¹¹ καὶ ἐμοὶ εὔχρηστον,¹² 12 ὃν ἀνέπεμψά¹³ ⟨σοι αὐτόν¹⁴, τοῦτ᾽¹⁵ ἔστιν τὰ ἐμὰ σπλάγχνα¹⁶⟩· 13 ὃν ἐγὼ ἐβουλόμην¹⁷

---

1   TH: *such a one as, one such as*. Idiomatically, *being an old man*.
2   πρεσβύτης, ου, ὁ, *elder*, **old man**. app. to Παῦλος. Some interpret this word as if it was its homonym πρεσβευτής, *ambassador* (as RSV). There is no textual evidence for this reading.
3   νυνί, adv. *now, at this moment*, an emphatic form of νῦν strengthened by ι demonstrative.
4   TH: ascensive or additive καί *also, even*.
5   δέσμιος, ου, ὁ, *prisoner, captive*.
6   δεσμός, ου, ὁ, *bond, chain*, **imprisonment**.
7   Ὀνήσιμος, ου, ὁ, *Onesimus*. TH: in app. to ὅν, *whom I birthed (namely) Onesimus*.
8   ποτέ, adv. *then*.
9   ἄχρηστος, ον, adj. *useless, worthless*. TH: subst. adj. with τόν in app. to Ὀνήσιμον, *the one useless*.
10 νυνί, adv. *now, at this moment*, emphatic form of νῦν strengthened by ι demonstrative.
11 NA²⁸ indicates some MSS read δὲ καὶ σοί.
12 εὔχρηστος, ον, adj. *useful*. TH: subst. adj. with τόν in app. to Ὀνήσιμον, *the one useful*.
13 ἀναπέμπω, *I send back*. MH: aor. act. indic. 1ˢᵗ sg. cmpd. ἀνέπεμψά = prep. + aug. + root + tense formative (ἀν + ἐ + πέμπ + σα). No per. ending in 1ˢᵗ sg.
14 TH: αὐτόν is redundant with ὅν, keeping the focus on *Onesimus*.
15 TH: The neut. sg. form refers probably to the "idea" of the previous clause (Paul sending Onesimus) or may result from the collective neut. pred. nom. τὰ ἐμὰ σπλάγχνα.
16 σπλάγχνον, ου, τό, *inward parts, intestines, viscera*, metaph. *heart*. TH: NA²⁸ indicates some MSS add προσλαβοῦ.
17 βούλομαι, *I wish, want, desire*. MH: impf. mid/pass. 1ˢᵗ sg. ἐβουλόμην = aug. + root + connecting vowel + secondary mid./pass. per. ending (ἐ + βουλ + ο + μην).

πρὸς ἐμαυτὸν¹ κατέχειν², ἵνα ὑπὲρ σοῦ 'μοι διακονῇ³⁾ ἐν τοῖς δεσμοῖς⁴ τοῦ εὐαγγελίου, 14 χωρὶς⁵ δὲ τῆς σῆς⁶ γνώμης⁷ οὐδὲν ἠθέλησα ποιῆσαι, ἵνα μὴ ὡς κατὰ ἀνάγκην⁸ τὸ ἀγαθόν σου ᾖ⁹ ἀλλὰ κατὰ ἑκούσιον¹⁰. 15 τάχα¹¹ γὰρ διὰ τοῦτο¹² ἐχωρίσθη¹³ πρὸς ὥραν¹⁴ ἵνα αἰώνιον αὐτὸν ἀπέχῃς¹⁵, 16 οὐκέτι¹⁶ ὡς δοῦλον ἀλλὰ ὑπὲρ¹⁷ δοῦλον, ἀδελφὸν ἀγαπητόν¹⁸, μάλιστα¹⁹ ἐμοί,

1 ἐμαυτοῦ, ῆς, reflex. pron. *myself.*
2 κατέχω, *I keep, hold on to, hold back, restrain.* TH: complementary inf. to ἐβουλόμην, *I want to keep.*
3 διακονέω, *I serve.* MH: pres. act. subj. 3rd sg. διακονῇ = root + lengthened connecting vowel contracts + per. ending (διακον + ῇ). TH: *he would serve.*
4 δεσμός, ου, ὁ, *bond, chain, imprisonment.*
5 χωρίς, prep. *apart from.*
6 σός, σή, σόν, adj. *your.*
7 γνώμη, ης, ἡ, *mind, purpose,* **consent.**
8 ἀνάγκη, ης, ἡ, *necessity, compulsion.*
9 MH: pres. act. subj. 3rd sg. of εἰμί. TH: subjunctive with ἵνα.
10 ἑκούσιος, α, ον, adj. *voluntary.* TH: *voluntarily.*
11 τάχα, adv. *perhaps, possibly.*
12 διὰ τοῦτο, TH: causal use of διά; on account of this, **for this reason.**
13 χωρίζω, *I separate, depart, leave.* MH: aor. pass. indic. 3rd, sg. ἐχωρίσθη = aug. + + tense formative (ἐ + χωριζ + θη) ζ changes to σ before θ. TH: divine pass.
14 TH: πρὸς ὥραν, *for a while.*
15 ἀπέχω, *I have back.* MH: pres. act. subj. 2nd sg. ἀπέχῃς = root + lengthened connecting vowel + per. ending (ἀπέχ + η + ς). TH: *you would have him back.*
16 οὐκέτι, adv. *no longer.* TH: μηκέτι would normally be expected following the subj. verb ἀπέχῃς.
17 TH: *over and above,* **more than.**
18 TH: app. to αἰώνιον αὐτὸν ... ὑπὲρ δοῦλον.
19 μάλιστα, adv. *especially.*

ΠΡΟΣ ΦΙΛΗΜΟΝΑ

πόσῳ¹ δὲ μᾶλλον σοὶ καὶ ἐν σαρκὶ καὶ ἐν κυρίῳ². 17 Εἰ οὖν με ἔχεις κοινωνόν³, προσλαβοῦ⁴ αὐτὸν ὡς ἐμέ. 18 εἰ δέ τι ἠδίκησέν⁵ σε ἢ ὀφείλει⁶, τοῦτο ἐμοὶ ⸂ἐλλόγα⁷· 19 ἐγὼ Παῦλος ἔγραψα τῇ ἐμῇ χειρί, ἐγὼ ἀποτίσω⁸· ἵνα μὴ⁹ λέγω σοι ὅτι καὶ¹⁰ σεαυτόν¹¹ μοι προσοφείλεις¹². 20 ναί¹³, ἀδελφέ, ἐγώ σου ὀναίμην¹⁴ ἐν κυρίῳ· ἀνάπαυσόν¹⁵ μου τὰ σπλάγχνα¹⁶ ἐν ⸂Χριστῷ. 21 πεποιθὼς¹⁷ τῇ ὑπακοῇ¹ σου ἔγραψά σοι, εἰδὼς² ὅτι

1 πόσος, η/ον, *how much, how many.*
2 TH: *both in (the) flesh and in (the) Lord.*
3 κοινωνός, ου, ὁ, *partner.*
4 προσλαμβάνω, *I welcome.* MH: sec. aor. mid. impv. 2ⁿᵈ sg. cmpd. προσλαβοῦ = root + secondary mid. ending (προσλαβ + ο + υ).
5 ἀδικέω, *I wrong, do wrong, injure.* MH: aor. act. ind. 3ʳᵈ sg.
6 ὀφείλω, *I owe, am indebted, ought, am obligated.*
7 ἐλλογέω, *I charge to one's account.* MH: pres. act. impv. 2ⁿᵈ sg. = ἐλλογε + ε (impv. 2ⁿᵈ sg) › ἔλλογα (epsilon contract verbs sometimes act like alpha contract verbs) + ε › ἐλλόγα (alpha contract vowel dominates epsilon ending).
8 ἀποτίνω, *I repay.* MH: fut. act. ind. 1st sg.
9 TH: ἵνα μὴ λέγω *lest* or *so that I not say* ...(expressing negative intention).
10 TH: ascensive or additive καί *also, even.*
11 σεαυτοῦ, ῆς, reflex. pron. *yourself.* TH: dir. obj. of προσοφείλεις, *you owe yourself to me.*
12 προσοφείλω, *I owe, owe besides.*
13 ναί, *yes.*
14 ὀνίνημι, *I have benefit of* or *I benefit from.* MH: aor. mid. opt. 1ˢᵗ sg. inter. ὀναίμην = aor. stem (root = ὀνη) + tense formative + secondary per ending (ὀνα + ι + μην). TH: voluntative opt., *might I have this benefit from you?*
15 ἀναπαύω, *I cause to rest, **refresh**.* MH: aor. act. impv. 2ⁿᵈ sg.
16 σπλάγχνον, ου, τό, *inward parts, intestines, viscera,* metaph. *heart.*
17 MH: perf. act. prtc. masc. nom. sg. from πείθω = πε (redup.) + ποιθ (stem change) + κως (perf. prtc. ending) › πεποιθὼς (κ assimilates to ϑ) and TH: causal adv. prtc., *since I am convinced, confident of.*

καὶ³ ὑπὲρ ⌜ἃ λέγω ποιήσεις. 22 ἅμα⁴ δὲ καὶ⁵ ἑτοίμαζέ⁶ μοι ξενίαν⁷, ἐλπίζω⁸ γὰρ ὅτι διὰ τῶν προσευχῶν⁹ ὑμῶν χαρισθήσομαι¹⁰ ὑμῖν.

23 ⌜Ἀσπάζεταί σε Ἐπαφρᾶς¹¹ ὁ συναιχμάλωτός¹² μου ἐν Χριστῷ Ἰησοῦ, 24 Μᾶρκος¹³, Ἀρίσταρχος¹⁴, Δημᾶς¹⁵, Λουκᾶς¹⁶, οἱ συνεργοί¹⁷ μου. 25 Ἡ χάρις τοῦ ⌜κυρίου¹⁸ Ἰησοῦ Χριστοῦ μετὰ τοῦ πνεύματος ⌜ὑμῶν.¹⁹

---

1 ὑπακοή, ῆς, ἡ, *obedience*. TH: dat. dir. obj. of πεποιθώς.
2 MH: pf. act. prtc. nom. 1ˢᵗ sg. from οἶδα, *I know*. οἶδα is already the pf. of εἴδω.
3 TH: ascensive or additive καί *also, even*.
4 ἅμα, adv. *at the same time, together*.
5 TH: ascensive or additive καί *also, even*.
6 ἑτοιμάζω, *I prepare, make or get ready, provide*. MH: pres. act. impv. 2ⁿᵈ sg.
7 ξενία, ας, ἡ, *hospitality, guest room*.
8 ἐλπίζω, *I hope, hope for, expect*.
9 προσευχή, ῆς, ἡ, *prayer, place of prayer*. MH: gen. fem. pl.
10 χαρίζομαι, *I give, grant, return*. MH: first fut. pass. indic. 1ˢᵗ sg. χαρισθήσομαι = root (χαριζ > χαρισ) + tense formative + connecting vowel + pass ending. (χαρισ + θησ + ο + μαι). TH: pass. *will be restored*.
11 Ἐπαφρᾶς, ᾶ, ὁ, *Epaphras*.
12 συναιχμάλωτος, ου, ὁ, *fellow-prisoner, fellow captive (of war*. lit. *taken with a spear)*. TH: app. to Ἐπαφρᾶς.
13 Μᾶρκος, ου, ὁ, *Mark*.
14 Ἀρίσταρχος, ου, ὁ, *Aristarchus*.
15 Δημᾶς, ᾶ, ὁ, *Demas*.
16 Λουκᾶς, ᾶ, ὁ, *Luke*.
17 συνεργός, ου, ὁ, *fellow-worker, co-worker, colleague*. TH: οἱ συνεργοί is nom. in app. to Μᾶρκος, Ἀρίσταρχος, Δημᾶς, and Λουκᾶς.
18 NA²⁸ indicates some MSS add ἡμῶν.
19 NA²⁸ indicates some MSS add Ἀμήν.

Appendices

APPENDIX I
SBLGNT APPARATUS
DIFFERENCES BETWEEN THE SBLGNT AND NA28

APPENDIX II
VOCABULARY 50 TIMES OR MORE SORTED BY FREQUENCY

APPENDIX III
VOCABULARY 50 TIMES OR MORE ARRANGED ALPHABETICALLY

APPENDIX IV
KOINĒ GREEK PARADIGM CHARTS

Appendix I

SBLGNT APPARATUS

ΠΡΟΣ ΚΟΛΟΣΣΑΕΙΣ

1:1 **Χριστοῦ Ἰησοῦ** WH Treg NIV] Ἰησοῦ Χριστοῦ RP
2 **Κολοσσαῖς** WH NIV] Κολασσαῖς Treg RP • ἡμῶν WH Treg NIV] + καὶ κυρίου Ἰησοῦ Χριστοῦ RP
3 **θεῷ** WH NIV] + καὶ Treg RP • περὶ WH NIV RP] ὑπὲρ Treg
4 ἣν ἔχετε WH Treg NIV] τὴν RP
6 κόσμῳ WH Treg NIV] + καὶ RP
7 καθὼς WH Treg NIV] + καὶ RP • ἡμῶν WH Treg NIV] ὑμῶν RP NA
10 περιπατῆσαι WH Treg NIV] + ὑμᾶς RP • τῇ ἐπιγνώσει WH Treg NIV] εἰς τὴν ἐπίγνωσιν RP
12 ὑμᾶς WH NIV] ἡμᾶς Treg RP
16 πάντα WH Treg NIV] + τὰ RP • καὶ WH NIV] + τὰ Treg RP
18 ἐστιν Treg NIV RP] + ἡ WH
20 δι' αὐτοῦ WH RP NA] –Treg NIV• ἐν WH Treg NIV] ἐπὶ RP 22 ἀποκατηλλάγητε Holmes] ἀποκατήλλαξεν WH Treg NIV RP
23 πάσῃ WH Treg NIV]+ τῇ RP
26 νῦν WH Treg NIV] νυνὶ RP
27 ὅ WH Treg NIV] ὅς RP
28 **Χριστῷ** WH Treg NIV] + Ἰησοῦ RP

2:1 ὑπὲρ WH Treg NIV] περὶ RP
2 **συμβιβασθέντες** WH Treg NIV]

συμβιβασθέντων RP • πᾶν πλοῦτος WH NIV]
πᾶν τὸ πλοῦτος Treg; πάντα πλοῦτον RP • θεοῦ
WH Treg NIV] + καὶ πατρὸς καὶ τοῦ RP
3 καὶ WH Treg NIV] + τῆς RP
4 τοῦτο WH NIV]+ δὲ Treg RP • μηδεὶς WH Treg
NIV] μή τις RP
7 βεβαιούμενοι WH Treg NIV] + ἐν RP •
περισσεύοντες Treg NIV] + ἐν αὐτῇ WH RP
11 σώματος WH Treg NIV] + τῶν ἁμαρτιῶν RP
12 βαπτισμῷ Treg NIV] βαπτίσματι WH RP • ἐκ
WH Treg NIV] + τῶν RP
13 ἐν NIV RP] – WH Treg
16 ἢ Treg RP] καὶ WH NIV
17 τοῦ WH Treg NIV] – RP
18 ἃ WH Treg NIV] + μὴ RP

3:4 ὑμῶν Treg NIV] ἡμῶν WH RP
5 μέλη WH Treg NA] + ὑμῶν NIV RP
6 ἐπὶ τοὺς υἱοὺς τῆς ἀπειθείας RP NA] –WH Treg
NIV
7 τούτοις WH Treg NIV] αὐτοῖς RP
11 τὰ Treg NIV RP] – WH
13 κύριος WH Treg NIV] Χριστὸς RP
14 ὅ WH Treg NIV] ἥτις RP
15 Χριστοῦ WH Treg NIV] θεοῦ RP
16 ψαλμοῖς WH Treg NIV] + καὶ RP • ὕμνοις WH
Treg NIV] + καὶ RP • ἐν WH RP] + τῇ Treg NIV •
ταῖς καρδίαις WH Treg NIV] τῇ καρδίᾳ RP •
θεῷ WH Treg NIV] κυρίῳ RP
17 ὅτι Treg NIV RP] ὅτι WH • ἐὰν WH Treg NIV] ἂν
RP • θεῷ WH Treg NIV]+ καὶ RP
18 τοῖς WH Treg NIV] + ἰδίοις RP

20 εὐάρεστόν ἐστιν WH Treg NIV] ἐστιν εὐάρεστον RP 22 ὀφθαλμοδουλίαις WH Treg RP] ὀφθαλμοδουλίᾳ NIV • κύριον WH Treg NIV] θεόν RP
23 ὃ WH Treg NIV] καὶ πᾶν ὅ τι RP
24 ἀπολήμψεσθε WH Treg NIV] λήψεσθε RP • τῷ WH Treg NIV] + γὰρ RP
25 γὰρ WH Treg NIV] δὲ RP

4:1 οὐρανῷ WH Treg NIV] οὐρανοῖς RP
8 γνῶτε WH Treg NIV] γνῷ RP • ἡμῶν WH Treg NIV] ὑμῶν RP
12 Χριστοῦ RP] + Ἰησοῦ WH Treg NIV • σταθῆτε WH Treg NIV] στῆτε RP • πεπληροφορημένοι WH Treg NIV] πεπληρωμένοι RP
13 πολὺν πόνον WH Treg NIV] ζῆλον πολὺν RP
15 Νύμφαν καὶ ... οἶκον αὐτῆς WH NIV] Νυμφᾶν καὶ ... οἶκον αὐτῶν Treg; Νυμφᾶν καὶ ... οἶκον αὐτοῦ RP
16 Λαοδικέων WH Treg NIV] Λαοδικαίων RP
18 ὑμῶν WH Treg NIV] + Ἀμήν RP

ΠΡΟΣ ΦΙΛΗΜΟΝΑ

1:2 ἀδελφῇ WH Treg NIV] ἀγαπητῇ RP
5 πρὸς NIV RP] εἰς WH Treg
6 τοῦ WH NIV RP] – Treg • Χριστόν WH Treg NIV] + Ἰησοῦν RP
7 χαρὰν WH Treg NIV] Χάριν RP • πολλὴν ἔσχον WH Treg NIV] ἔχομεν πολλὴν RP
9 Χριστοῦ Ἰησοῦ WH Treg NIV] Ἰησοῦ Χριστοῦ RP

10 δεσμοῖς WH Treg NIV] + μου RP
11 δὲ WH Treg RP] + καὶ NIV
12 σοι αὐτόν ... σπλάγχνα WH Treg NIV] σὺ δὲ αὐτόν ... σπλάγχνα προσλαβοῦ RP
13 μοι διακονῇ WH Treg NIV] διακονῇ μοι RP
18 ἐλλόγα WH Treg NIV] ἐλλόγει RP
20 Χριστῷ WH Treg NIV] κυρίῳ RP
21 ἃ WH Treg NIV] ὃ RP
23 Ἀσπάζεταί WH Treg NIV] Ἀσπάζονταί RP
25 κυρίου WH NIV] + ἡμῶν Treg RP • ὑμῶν WH Treg NIV] + Ἀμήν RP

DIFFERENCES BETWEEN THE SBLGNT AND NA28

A. DIFFERENCES IN WORDING/SPELLING. SBLGNT] NA28

Colossians
  1:7 ὑπὲρ ἡμῶν] ὑπὲρ ὑμῶν
  1:22 ἀποκατηλλάγητε] ἀποκατήλλαξεν
  2:16 ἢ ἐν πόσει] καὶ ἐν πόσει
  2:16 νουμηνίας] νεομηνίας
  3:16 ἐν χάριτι] ἐν [τῇ] χάριτι
  3:22 ὀφθαλμοδουλίαις,] ὀφθαλμοδουλίᾳ
  4:12 δοῦλος Χριστοῦ,] δοῦλος Χριστοῦ [Ἰησοῦ]

Philemon
  11 νυνὶ δὲ σοὶ] νυνὶ δὲ [καὶ] σοὶ
  16 ἀλλὰ ὑπὲρ δοῦλον] ἀλλ' ὑπὲρ δοῦλον

APPENDIX I: SBLGNT APPARATUS

B. Punctuation Differences in Col 1-2. SBLGNT] NA28

Colossians
1:2 ἐν Χριστῷ·] ἐν Χριστῷ,
1:9 αἰτούμενοι ἵνα] αἰτούμενοι, ἵνα
1:10 ἀρεσκείαν ἐν παντὶ] ἀρεσκείαν, ἐν παντὶ
1:11 μετὰ χαρᾶς,] . Μετὰ χαρᾶς
1:12 ἐν τῷ φωτί,] ἐν τῷ φωτί·
1:20 τὰ ἐν τοῖς οὐρανοῖς·] τὰ ἐν τοῖς οὐρανοῖς.
1:21 τοῖς πονηροῖς—] τοῖς πονηροῖς,
1:22 διὰ τοῦ θανάτου—] διὰ τοῦ θανάτου
1:26 ἀπὸ τῶν γενεῶν,—] ἀπὸ τῶν γενεῶν-
2:2 αὐτῶν,] αὐτῶν
2:4 τοῦτο λέγω] Τοῦτο λέγω,
2:10-11 ἐξουσίας, [11]ἐν ᾧ] ἐξουσίας. [11]Ἐν ᾧ
2:13 σὺν αὐτῷ·] σὺν αὐτῷ.
2:13 τὰ παραπτώματα,] τὰ παραπτώματα.
2:16 σαββάτων,] σαββάτων·
2:20 δογματίζεσθε·] δογματίζεσθε;
2:21 Μὴ] μὴ
2:22 ἀνθρώπων;] ἀνθρώπων,

APPENDIX II
VOCABULARY 50 TIMES OR MORE SORTED BY FREQUENCY

19796	ὁ, ἡ, τό	the; (sub.) he, she, thing
8984	καί	and; (adv.) also, even
5569	αὐτός, ή, ό	he, she, it; (adj.) -self, same
2899	σύ, σοῦ; ὑμεῖς, ὑμῶν	you; you all
2777	δέ	but, rather, and, now
2737	ἐν	(+dat) in, with, among
2582	ἐγώ, (ἐ)μοῦ; ἡμεῖς, ἡμῶν	I; we
2458	εἰμί	I am, exist, happen
2352	λέγω	I say, speak, claim
1857	εἰς	(+acc) to, into
1621	οὐ, οὐκ, οὐχ	not, no
1407	ὅς, ἥ, ὅ	who, which, that
1387	οὗτος, αὕτη, τοῦτο	this; (sub.) he, she, this one
1307	θεός, οῦ, ὁ and ἡ	God, god, divine one
1294	ὅτι	because, that
1243	πᾶς, πᾶσα, πᾶν	every, each, all, whole
1039	γάρ	for, because, since
1038	μή	not, no; (+subj.) in order that...not
913	ἐκ, ἐξ	(+gen) from, out from
911	Ἰησοῦς, οῦ, ὁ	Joshua, Jesus
887	ἐπί	(+gen/dat/acc) on, near, toward
714	κύριος, ου, ὁ	Lord, master, owner
707	ἔχω	I have, am
698	πρός	(+acc) to, toward, with
667	γίνομαι	I am, become, happen
666	διά	(+gen) through; (+acc) because of
663	ἵνα	so that, in order that
645	ἀπό	(+gen) from, away from
638	ἀλλά	but, yet, rather
633	ἔρχομαι	I come, go
568	ποιέω	I make, do
551	τίς, τί	who? which? what?
550	ἄνθρωπος, ου, ὁ	man, human
534	τις, τι	someone, something
528	Χριστός, οῦ, ὁ	Messiah, Anointed One, Christ

APPENDICES

504	ὡς	as, like
502	εἰ	if, whether
495	οὖν	therefore, then
470	κατά	(+gen) against, down; (+acc) according to
470	μετά	(+gen) with; (+acc) after, behind
453	ὁράω	I see, perceive, experience
428	ἀκούω	I hear, obey, listen
415	πολύς, πολλή, πολύ	much, many
415	δίδωμι	I give, entrust
413	πατήρ, πατρός, ὁ	father
389	ἡμέρα, ας, ἡ	day, time
379	πνεῦμα, ατος, τό	spirit, breath
375	υἱός, οῦ, ὁ	son
346	ἤ	or, than
344	εἷς	one, single
342	ἀδελφός, οῦ, ὁ	brother
332	περί	(+gen) concerning; (+acc) around
330	ἐάν	if, whenever
330	λόγος, ου, ὁ	word, speech, matter
330	ἐάν	if, whenever
321	ἑαυτοῦ, ῆς, οῦ	himself, herself, itself
320	οἶδα	I know, understand
297	λαλέω	I speak
273	οὐρανός, οῦ, ὁ	sky, heaven
262	μαθητής, οῦ, ὁ	disciple, student
258	λαμβάνω	I take, receive
250	γῆ, γῆς, ἡ	land, earth
243	ἐκεῖνος, η, ο	that; (sub.) he, she, that one
243	μέγας, μεγάλη, μέγα	large, great
242	πίστις, εως, ἡ	belief, faith, trust
241	πιστεύω	I believe, trust
233	ἅγιος, ία, ον	holy, pure, devout; (sub.) Saint
232	ἀποκρίνομαι	I answer
229	ὄνομα, ατος, τό	name
227	οὐδείς, οὐδεμία, οὐδέν	no; (sub.) no one, nothing
221	γινώσκω	I know, understand, learn
221	ὑπό	(+gen) by; (+acc) underneath
217	ἐξέρχομαι	I go out, exit

APPENDIX II: VOCABULARY 50 TIMES OR MORE SORTED BY FREQUENCY

216	ἀνήρ, ἀνδρός, ὁ	man, husband
216	γυνή, αικός, ἡ	woman, wife
213	τέ	and, so
209	δύναμαι	I am able
208	θέλω	I wish, want
207	οὕτω/οὕτως	thus, so
200	ἰδού	Look!, Notice!, See!
195	Ἰουδαῖος, αία, αῖον	Jewish; (sub.) Jew
194	νόμος, ου, ὁ	law, custom
193	εἰσέρχομαι	I go into, enter
193	παρά	(+gen) along side, from; (+dat) beside, near; (+acc) out from, by
192	γράφω	I write
185	κόσμος, ου, ὁ	world, universe, order
182	καθώς	as, just as
178	μέν	however, but, indeed
176	χείρ, χειρός, ἡ	hand
176	εὑρίσκω	I find, discover
175	ἄγγελος, ου, ὁ	messenger, envoy, angel
174	ὄχλος, ου, ὁ	crowd, multitude
172	ἁμαρτία, ίας, ἡ	sin, guilt, failure
170	ἄν	[conditional particle] (Not Translated—indicates possibility but not certainty)
169	ἔργον, ου, τό	work, accomplishment
165	δόξα, ης, ἡ	splendor, glory; reputation
163	πόλις, εως, ἡ	town, city
162	βασιλεία, ας, ἡ	kingdom, providence, dominion
160	ἔθνος, ους, τό	nation, culture group, people
159	τότε	at that time, then
158	ἐσθίω	I eat, drink, consume
158	Παῦλος, ου, ὁ	Paul
156	καρδία, ας, ἡ	heart
156	Πέτρος, ου, ὁ	Peter
155	πρῶτος, η, ον	first, most prominent
155	χάρις, ιτος, ἡ	grace, thankfulness, kindness
154	ἄλλος, η, ο	other, another
154	ἵστημι	I set, place, establish
153	πορεύομαι	I go, walk

83

APPENDICES

150	ὑπέρ	*(+gen) on behalf of, for; (+acc) over, beyond*
148	καλέω	*I call, summon, invite*
147	σάρξ, σαρκός, ἡ	*flesh, muscle, body*
145	νῦν	*now, currently, presently*
145	ἕως	*while, until, up to the point of, as far as*
144	ὅστις, ἥτις, ὅ τι	*whoever, whichever, any one who*
144	προφήτης, ου, ὁ	*prophet*
143	ἐγείρω	*I rise, raise*
143	ἀγαπάω	*I love, adore*
143	ἀφίημι	*I release, dissolve, reprieve, depart*
143	οὐδέ	*but not, nor, neither*
142	λαός, οῦ, ὁ	*people, populace, multitude*
142	σῶμα, ατος, τό	*body*
141	πάλιν	*again*
140	ζάω	*I live*
139	φωνή, ῆς, ἡ	*voice, sound, communication*
135	δύο	*two*
135	ζωή, ῆς, ἡ	*life, existence*
135	Ἰωάν(ν)ης, ου, ὁ	*John*
133	βλέπω	*I see, observe, notice*
131	ἀποστέλλω	*I send (off)*
129	σύν	*(+dat) with, along with*
128	ἀμήν	*certainly, truly, indeed*
128	νεκρός, ά, όν	*dead*
126	δοῦλος, ου, ὁ	*slave, bondservant*
123	ὅταν	*whenever, when*
122	αἰών, ῶνος, ὁ	*age, era, lifetime*
122	ἀρχιερεύς, έως, ὁ	*high priest, chief priest*
122	βάλλω	*I throw, place*
120	θάνατος, ου, ὁ	*death*
119	δύναμις, εως, ἡ	*power, strength, ability*
119	παραδίδωμι	*I hand over, deliver, grant*
118	μένω	*I remain, continue*
117	ἀπέρχομαι	*I depart, go away*
117	ζητέω	*I seek, search, inquire*
116	ἀγάπη, ης, ἡ	*love, adoration*
115	βασιλεύς, έως, ὁ	*king*
115	κρίνω	*I judge, decide, choose*

APPENDIX II: VOCABULARY 50 TIMES OR MORE SORTED BY FREQUENCY

114	ἐκκλησία, ας, ἡ	assembly, gathering, community, church
114	ἴδιος, ία, ον	one's own
113	μόνος, η, ον	alone, only
113	οἶκος, ου, ὁ	house, dwelling, family
111	ἀποθνήσκω	I die, perish
111	ὅσος, η, ον	as many as, as much as, as great as
109	ἀλήθεια, ας, ἡ	truth, reality
109	μέλλω	I am about to, mean to
109	παρακαλέω	I encourage, call, request
108	ὅλος, η, ον	whole, entire
108	ἀνίστημι	I raise, resurrect, establish
106	σῴζω	I save, rescue, keep safe
106	ὥρα, ας, ἡ	hour, time, period, season
105	πῶς	how?
102	ὅτε	when
102	ψυχή, ῆς, ἡ	soul, life
102	ἐξουσία, ας, ἡ	authority, capability
101	ἀγαθός, ή, όν	good, beneficial
101	αἴρω	I lift up, raise up, take away
101	δεῖ	I must, am required, ought
101	ὁδός, οῦ, ἡ	road, way, path, trip
101	καλός, ή, όν	beautiful, good, noble
100	ἀλλήλων	one another
100	ὀφθαλμός, οῦ,	eye
100	τίθημι	I put, place, lay
99	τέκνον, ου, τό	child
97	ἕτερος, α, ον	other, another
97	Φαρισαῖος, ου, ὁ	Pharisee, Separatist
97	αἷμα, ατος, τό	blood, bloodshed
97	ἄρτος, ου, ὁ	bread, food
97	γεννάω	I beget, give birth, parent
97	διδάσκω	I teach, instruct
95	ἐκεῖ	there
95	περιπατέω	I walk (about), live, behave
95	φοβέω	I fear, respect, flee frightened
94	ἐνώπιον	before, face to face, in the view of
94	τόπος, ου, ὁ	place, position
93	ἔτι	yet, still, even now

85

APPENDICES

93	οἰκία, ας, ἡ	house, building, family
93	πούς, ποδός, ὁ	foot
91	δικαιοσύνη, ης, ἡ	righteousness, justice
91	εἰρήνη, ης, ἡ	peace, well-being
91	θάλασσα, ης, ἡ	lake, sea
91	κάθημαι	I sit, settle, reside
91	μηδείς, μηδεμία, μηδέν	no, no one, nothing
90	ἀπόλλυμι	ruin, destroy, perish
90	πίπτω	I fall, collapse
89	ἀκολουθέω	I follow, obey
88	ἑπτά	seven
87	οὔτε	and not, nor, neither
86	ἄρχω	I rule, lead, begin
86	πληρόω	I fill, complete, fulfill
85	προσέρχομαι	I go to, visit, approach
85	καιρός, οῦ, ὁ	time, period, season
85	προσεύχομαι	I pray, petition a deity
83	κἀγώ	and I, I too (crasis καὶ ἐγώ)
83	μήτηρ, τρός, ἡ	mother
83	ὥστε	so that, therefore, consequently
82	ἕκαστος, η, ον	every, each
81	ἀναβαίνω	I go up, ascend
81	ὅπου	where, whereas, whenever
81	ἐκβάλλω	I throw out, expel, reject
81	μᾶλλον	more, exceedingly, rather
80	καταβαίνω	I go down, descend
80	Μωϋσῆς	Moses
79	ἀπόστολος, ου, ὁ	delegate, ambassador, apostle
79	δίκαιος, αία, ον	just, righteous, fair
79	πέμπω	I send, despatch
79	ὑπάγω	I withdraw, go away
78	πονηρός, ά, όν	evil, bad, worthless, sick
78	στόμα, ατος, τό	mouth, opening
77	ἀνοίγω	I open
77	βαπτίζω	I soak, submerge, wash
77	Ἰερουσαλήμ	Jerusalem
77	σημεῖον, ου, τό	sign, mark, signal, miracle
76	μαρτυρέω	I give evidence, witness, testify

APPENDIX II: VOCABULARY 50 TIMES OR MORE SORTED BY FREQUENCY

76	πρόσωπον, ου, τό	face, appearance, expression, presence
76	ὕδωρ, ατος, τό	water, rain
75	εὐαγγέλιον, ου, τό	good news, gospel
75	δώδεκα	twelve
75	κεφαλή, ῆς, ἡ	head
75	Σίμων, ωνος, ὁ	Simon
74	ἀποκτείνω, ἀποκτέννω	I kill, slay
74	χαίρω	I am glad, rejoice, welcome
73	Ἀβραάμ, ὁ	Abraham
72	πίνω	I drink
72	φῶς, φωτός, τό	light, torch
72	ἱερόν, οῦ, τό	temple, holy place
71	πῦρ, ός, τό	fire
71	τηρέω	I watch over, guard, keep
70	αἰτέω	I ask, demand
69	αἰώνιος, ον	long-lasting, eternal
69	ἄγω	I lead, carry, arrest, observe
68	ἐμός, ή, όν	my, mine
68	τρεῖς, τρία	three
68	Ἰσραήλ, ὁ	Israel
68	σάββατον, ου, τό	Sabbath
67	ῥῆμα, ατος, τό	word, saying, thing
67	πιστός, ή, όν	faithful, trustworthy, believing
67	πλοῖον, ου, τό	boat, ship, vessel
67	ἀπολύω	I release, pardon, dismiss
66	ἐντολή, ῆς, ἡ	command, order, commandment
66	καρπός, ου, ὁ	fruit, produce, profit
66	φέρω	I carry, bring, lead
65	φημί	I declare, say
65	εἴτε	if, either, or, whether
63	γραμματεύς, έως, ὁ	scribe, law expert, high official
63	δαιμόνιον, ου, τό	demon, evil spirit, inferior divinity
63	ἐρωτάω	I ask, inquire, question
63	ὄρος, ους, τό	mountain, hill
62	ἔξω	outside, out
62	δοκέω	I think, suppose, form an opinion; I seem, suppose
62	θέλημα, ατος, τό	will, want

APPENDICES

62	θρόνος, ου, ὁ	chair, seat, throne
62	Ἱεροσόλυμα, τά and ἡ	Jerusalem (city or its inhabitants)
61	ἀγαπητός, ή, όν	beloved, dearly loved
61	Γαλιλαία, ας, ἡ	Galilee
61	δοξάζω	I honor, exalt, glorify
61	κηρύσσω	I preach, proclaim, announce
61	νύξ, νυκτός, ἡ	night (often metaph.)
61	ὧδε	here, thus, in this way, exceedingly so
60	ἤδη	already, now; by this time
60	ἱμάτιον, ου, τό	garment; outer garment
60	προσκυνέω	I worship; I fall down in worship, prostrate myself
60	ὑπάρχω	I am present, at one's disposal; I am, exist
59	ἀσπάζομαι	I greet, welcome
59	Δαυίδ, ὁ	David
59	διδάσκαλος, ου, ὁ	teacher, master
59	λίθος, ου, ὁ	stone
59	συνάγω	I gather together, collect; receive as a guest
59	χαρά, ᾶς, ἡ	joy, delight, gladness
59	εὐθύς, εῖα, ύ	immediately, straight, proper
58	θεωρέω	I view (as a spectator), behold, observe, see
58	μέσος, η, ον	middle, in the midst
57	τοιοῦτος, αύτη, οῦτον	such as this, of such a kind
56	δέχομαι	I take, receive; welcome
56	ἐπερωτάω	I ask, inquire
56	μηδέ	but not, nor; not even, not either
56	συναγωγή, ῆς, ἡ	assembly, gathering; synagogue
56	τρίτος, η, ον	third
55	ἀρχή, ῆς, ἡ	begining; power; ruler
55	κράζω	call out, cry out, scream
55	λοιπός, ή, όν	rest, remaining; from now on
55	Πιλᾶτος, ου, ὁ	Pilate
54	δεξιός, ά, όν	right (directional; often metph.); true
54	εὐαγγελίζω	bring/proclaim (the) good news
54	οὐχί	not, no, in no way (intensified οὐ)
53	χρόνος, ου, ὁ	time, occasion,

APPENDIX II: VOCABULARY 50 TIMES OR MORE SORTED BY FREQUENCY

53	διό	therefore, for this reason
53	ἐλπίς, ίδος, ἡ	expectation, hope
53	ὅπως	how; in order that
52	ἐπαγγελία, ας, ἡ	promise, offer
52	ἔσχατος, η, ον	last, farthest, least
52	παιδίον, ου, τό	child; young servent/slave
52	πείθω	persuade, win over; depend on
52	σπείρω	sow seed, scatter
51	σοφία, ας, ἡ	wisdom, sound judgement
50	γλῶσσα, ης, ἡ	tongue; language; joyful speech
50	κακός, ή, όν	evil, bad; incorrect
50	μακάριος, ία, ιον	favored, blessed
50	παραβολή, ῆς, ἡ	parable, illustration; type, embodiment
50	τυφλός, ή, όν	blind (often metaph.)
49	γραφή, ῆς, ἡ	scripture, writing[1]

---

[1] Though γραγή occurs 49 times in the SBLGNT, this word occurs 50 times in the NA. As such, many resources include γραφή in their most frequently occurring word list and retention requirements. To retain this standard, it has also been included in this most frequently occurring vocabulary list. Γραγή is not included in the General Reader's footnotes or chapter vocabulary helps.

89

Appendix III

Vocabulary 50 Times or More Arranged Alphabetically

Α α

Ἀβραάμ, ὁ	Abraham
ἀγαθός, ή, όν	good, beneficial
ἀγαπάω	I love, adore
ἀγάπη, ης, ἡ	love, adoration
ἀγαπητός, ή, όν	beloved, dearly loved
ἄγγελος, ου, ὁ	messenger, envoy, angel
ἅγιος, ία, ον	holy, pure, devout; (sub.) Saint
ἄγω	I lead, carry, arrest, observe
ἀδελφός, οῦ, ὁ	brother
αἷμα, ατος, τό	blood, bloodshed
αἴρω	I lift up, raise up, take away
αἰτέω	I ask, demand
αἰών, ῶνος, ὁ	age, era, lifetime
αἰώνιος, ον	long-lasting, eternal
ἀκολουθέω	I follow, obey
ἀκούω	I hear, obey, listen
ἀλήθεια, ας, ἡ	truth, reality
ἀλλά	but, yet, rather
ἀλλήλων	one another
ἄλλος, η, ο	other, another
ἁμαρτία, ίας, ἡ	sin, guilt, failure
ἀμήν	certainly, truly, indeed
ἄν	[conditional particle] (Not Translated - indicates possibility but not certainty)
ἀναβαίνω	I go up, ascend
ἀνήρ, ἀνδρός, ὁ	man, husband
ἄνθρωπος, ου, ὁ	man, human
ἀνίστημι	I raise, resurrect, establish
ἀνοίγω	I open
ἀπέρχομαι	I depart, go away
ἀπό	(+gen) from, away from
ἀποθνήσκω	I die, perish

ἀποκρίνομαι	I answer
ἀποκτείνω, ἀποκτέννω	I kill, slay
ἀπόλλυμι	ruin, destroy, perish
ἀπολύω	I release, pardon, dismiss
ἀποστέλλω	I send (off)
ἀπόστολος, ου, ὁ	delegate, ambassador, apostle
ἄρτος, ου, ὁ	bread, food
ἀρχή, ῆς, ἡ	begining; power; ruler
ἀρχιερεύς, έως, ὁ	high priest, chief priest
ἄρχω	I rule, lead, begin
ἀσπάζομαι	I greet, welcome
αὐτός, ή, ὁ	he, she, it; (adj.) -self, same
ἀφίημι	I release, dissolve, reprieve, depart

Β β

βάλλω	I throw, place
βαπτίζω	I soak, submerge, wash
βασιλεία, ας, ἡ	kingdom, providence, dominion
βασιλεύς, έως, ὁ	king
βλέπω	I see, observe, notice

Γ γ

Γαλιλαία, ας, ἡ	Galilee
γάρ	for, because, since
γεννάω	I beget, give birth, parent
γῆ, γῆς, ἡ	land, earth
γίνομαι	I am, become, happen
γινώσκω	I know, understand, learn
γλῶσσα, ης, ἡ	tongue; language; joyful speech
γραμματεύς, έως, ὁ	scribe, law expert, high official
γραφή, ῆς, ἡ	scripture, writing
γράφω	I write
γυνή, αικός, ἡ	woman, wife

Δ δ

δαιμόνιον, ου, τό	demon, evil spirit, inferior divinity
Δαυίδ, ὁ	David
δέ	but, rather, and, now
δεῖ	I must, am required, ought
δεξιός, ά, όν	right (directional; often metph.); true
δέχομαι	I take, receive; welcome
διά	(+gen) through; (+acc) because of
διδάσκαλος, ου, ὁ	teacher, master
διδάσκω	I teach, instruct
δίδωμι	I give, entrust
δίκαιος, αία, ον	just, righteous, fair
δικαιοσύνη, ης, ἡ	righteousness, justice
διό	therefore, for this reason
δοκέω	I think, suppose, form an opinion; I seem, suppose
δόξα, ης, ἡ	splendor, glory; reputation
δοξάζω	I honor, exalt, glorify
δοῦλος, ου, ὁ	slave, bondservant
δύναμαι	I am able
δύναμις, εως, ἡ	power, strength, ability
δύο	two
δώδεκα	twelve

Ε ε

ἐάν	if, whenever
ἐάν	if, whenever
ἑαυτοῦ, ῆς, οῦ	himself, herself, itself
ἐγείρω	I rise, raise
ἐγώ, (ἐ)μοῦ; ἡμεῖς, ἡμῶν	I; we
ἔθνος, ους, τό	nation, culture group, people
εἰ	if, whether
εἰμί	I am, exist, happen
εἰρήνη, ης, ἡ	peace, well-being

εἷς	one, single
εἰς	(+acc) to, into
εἰσέρχομαι	I go into, enter
εἴτε	if, either, or, whether
ἐκ, ἐξ	(+gen) from, out from
ἕκαστος, η, ον	every, each
ἐκβάλλω	I throw out, expel, reject
ἐκεῖ	there
ἐκεῖνος, η, ο	that; (sub.) he, she, that one
ἐκκλησία, ας, ἡ	assembly, gathering, community, church
ἐλπίς, ίδος, ἡ	expectation, hope
ἐμός, ή, όν	my, mine
ἐν	(+dat) in, with, among
ἐντολή, ῆς, ἡ	command, order, commandment
ἐνώπιον	before, face to face, in the view of
ἐξέρχομαι	I go out, exit
ἐξουσία, ας, ἡ	authority, capability
ἔξω	outside, out
ἐπαγγελία, ας, ἡ	promise, offer
ἐπερωτάω	I ask, inquire
ἐπί	(+gen/dat/acc) on, near, toward
ἑπτά	seven
ἔργον, ου, τό	work, accomplishment
ἔρχομαι	I come, go
ἐρωτάω	I ask, inquire, question
ἐσθίω	I eat, drink, consume
ἔσχατος, η, ον	last, farthest, least
ἕτερος, α, ον	other, another
ἔτι	yet, still, even now
εὐαγγελίζω	bring/proclaim (the) good news
εὐαγγέλιον, ου, τό	good news, gospel
εὐθύς, εῖα, ύ	immediately, straight, proper
εὑρίσκω	I find, discover
ἔχω	I have, am
ἕως	while, until, up to the point of, as far as

APPENDIX III: VOCABULARY 50 TIMES OR MORE ARRANGED ALPHABETICALLY

Ζ ζ

ζάω	I live
ζητέω	I seek, search, inquire
ζωή, ῆς, ἡ	life, existence

Η η

ἤ	or, than
ἤδη	already, now; by this time
ἡμέρα, ας, ἡ	day, time

Θ ϑ

θάλασσα, ης, ἡ	lake, sea
θάνατος, ου, ὁ	death
θέλημα, ατος, τό	will, want
θέλω	I wish, want
θεός, οῦ, ὁ and ἡ	God, god, divine one
θεωρέω	I view (as a spectator), behold, observe, see
θρόνος, ου, ὁ	chair, seat, throne

Ι ι

ἴδιος, ία, ον	one's own
ἰδού	Look!, Notice!, See!
ἱερόν, οῦ, τό	temple, holy place
Ἱεροσόλυμα, τά and ἡ	Jerusalem (city or its inhabitants)
Ἱερουσαλήμ	Jerusalem
Ἰησοῦς, οῦ, ὁ	Joshua, Jesus
ἱμάτιον, ου, τό	garment; outer garment
ἵνα	so that, in order that

Ἰουδαῖος, αία, αῖον   Jewish; (sub.) Jew
Ἰσραήλ, ὁ   Israel
ἵστημι   I set, place, establish
Ἰωάν(ν)ης, ου, ὁ   John

Κ κ

κἀγώ   and I, I too (crasis καὶ ἐγώ)
κάθημαι   I sit, settle, reside
καθώς   as, just as
καί   and; (adv.) also, even
καιρός, οῦ, ὁ   time, period, season
κακός, ή, όν   evil, bad; incorrect
καλέω   I call, summon, invite
καλός, ή, όν   beautiful, good, noble
καρδία, ας, ἡ   heart
καρπός, ου, ὁ   fruit, produce, profit
κατά   (+gen) against, down; (+acc) according to
καταβαίνω   I go down, descend
κεφαλή, ῆς, ἡ   head
κηρύσσω   I preach, proclaim, announce
κόσμος, ου, ὁ   world, universe, order
κράζω   call out, cry out, scream
κρίνω   I judge, decide, choose
κύριος, ου, ὁ   Lord, master, owner

Λ λ

λαλέω   I speak
λαμβάνω   I take, receive
λαός, οῦ, ὁ   people, populace, multitude
λέγω   I say, speak, claim
λίθος, ου, ὁ   stone
λόγος, ου, ὁ   word, speech, matter
λοιπός, ή, όν   rest, remaining; from now on

APPENDIX III: VOCABULARY 50 TIMES OR MORE ARRANGED ALPHABETICALLY

Μ μ

μαθητής, οῦ, ὁ	disciple, student
μακάριος, ία, ιον	favored, blessed
μᾶλλον	more, exceedingly, rather
μαρτυρέω	I give evidence, witness, testify
μέγας, μεγάλη, μέγα	large, great
μέλλω	I am about to, mean to
μέν	however, but, indeed
μένω	I remain, continue
μέσος, η, ον	middle, in the midst
μετά	(+gen) with; (+acc) after, behind
μή	not, no; (+subj.) in order that...not
μηδέ	but not, nor; not even, not either
μηδείς, μηδεμία, μηδέν	no, no one, nothing
μήτηρ, τρός, ἡ	mother
μόνος, η, ον	alone, only
Μωϋσῆς	Moses

Ν ν

νεκρός, ά, όν	dead
νόμος, ου, ὁ	law, custom
νῦν	now, currently, presently
νύξ, νυκτός, ἡ	night (often metaph.)

Ο ο

ὁ, ἡ, τό	the; (sub.) he, she, thing
ὁδός, οῦ, ἡ	road, way, path, trip
οἶδα	I know, understand
οἰκία, ας, ἡ	house, building, family
οἶκος, ου, ὁ	house, dwelling, family
ὅλος, η, ον	whole, entire

ὄνομα, ατος, τό	name
ὅπου	where, whereas, whenever
ὅπως	how; in order that
ὁράω	I see, perceive, experience
ὄρος, ους, τό	mountain, hill
ὅς, ἥ, ὅ	who, which, that
ὅσος, η, ον	as many as, as much as, as great as
ὅστις, ἥτις, ὅ τι	whoever, whichever, any one who
ὅταν	whenever, when
ὅτε	when
ὅτι	because, that
οὐ, οὐκ, οὐχ	not, no
οὐδέ	but not, nor, neither
οὐδείς, οὐδεμία, οὐδέν	no; (sub.) no one, nothing
οὖν	therefore, then
οὐρανός, οῦ, ὁ	sky, heaven
οὔτε	and not, nor, neither
οὗτος, αὕτη, τοῦτο	this; (sub.) he, she, this one
οὕτω/οὕτως	thus, so
οὐχί	not, no, in no way (intensified οὐ)
ὀφθαλμός, οῦ,	eye
ὄχλος, ου, ὁ	crowd, multitude

Π π

παιδίον, ου, τό	child; young servent/slave
πάλιν	again
παρά	(+gen) along side, from; (+dat) beside, near; (+acc) out from, by
παραβολή, ῆς, ἡ	parable, illustration; type, embodiment
παραδίδωμι	I hand over, deliver, grant
παρακαλέω	I encourage, call, request
πᾶς, πᾶσα, πᾶν	every, each, all, whole
πατήρ, πατρός, ὁ	father
Παῦλος, ου, ὁ	Paul
πείθω	persuade, win over; depend on
πέμπω	I send, despatch

περί	(+gen) concerning; (+acc) around
περιπατέω	I walk (about), live, behave
Πέτρος, ου, ὁ	Peter
Πιλᾶτος, ου, ὁ	Pilate
πίνω	I drink
πίπτω	I fall, collapse
πιστεύω	I believe, trust
πίστις, εως, ἡ	belief, faith, trust
πιστός, ή, όν	faithful, trustworthy, believing
πληρόω	I fill, complete, fulfill
πλοῖον, ου, τό	boat, ship, vessel
πνεῦμα, ατος, τό	spirit, breath
ποιέω	I make, do
πόλις, εως, ἡ	town, city
πολύς, πολλή, πολύ	much, many
πονηρός, ά, όν	evil, bad, worthless, sick
πορεύομαι	I go, walk
πούς, ποδός, ὁ	foot
πρός	(+acc) to, toward, with
προσέρχομαι	I go to, visit, approach
προσεύχομαι	I pray, petition a deity
προσκυνέω	I worship; I fall down in worship, prostrate myself
πρόσωπον, ου, τό	face, appearance, expression, presence
προφήτης, ου, ὁ	prophet
πρῶτος, η, ον	first, most prominent
πῦρ, ός, τό	fire
πῶς	how?

Ρ ρ

ῥῆμα, ατος, τό	word, saying, thing

APPENDICES

Σ σ

σάββατον, ου, τό	Sabbath
σάρξ, σαρκός, ἡ	flesh, muscle, body
σημεῖον, ου, τό	sign, mark, signal, miracle
Σίμων, ωνος, ὁ	Simon
σοφία, ας, ἡ	wisdom, sound judgement
σπείρω	sow seed, scatter
στόμα, ατος, τό	mouth, opening
σύ, σοῦ; ὑμεῖς, ὑμῶν	you; you all
σύν	(+dat) with, along with
συνάγω	I gather together, collect; receive as a guest
συναγωγή, ῆς, ἡ	assembly, gathering; synagogue
σῴζω	I save, rescue, keep safe
σῶμα, ατος, τό	body

Τ τ

τέ	and, so
τέκνον, ου, τό	child
τηρέω	I watch over, guard, keep
τίθημι	I put, place, lay
τις, τι	someone, something
τίς, τί	who? which? what?
τοιοῦτος, αύτη, οῦτον	such as this, of such a kind
τόπος, ου, ὁ	place, position
τότε	at that time, then
τρεῖς, τρία	three
τρίτος, η, ον	third
τυφλός, ή, όν	blind (often metaph.)

APPENDIX III: VOCABULARY 50 TIMES OR MORE ARRANGED ALPHABETICALLY

Υ υ

ὕδωρ, ατος, τό	water, rain
υἱός, οῦ, ὁ	son
ὑπάγω	I withdraw, go away
ὑπάρχω	I am present, at one's disposal; I am, exist
ὑπέρ	(+gen) on behalf of, for; (+acc) over, beyond
ὑπό	(+gen) by; (+acc) underneath

Φ φ

Φαρισαῖος, ου, ὁ	Pharisee, Separatist
φέρω	I carry, bring, lead
φημί	I declare, say
φοβέω	I fear, respect, flee frightened
φωνή, ῆς, ἡ	voice, sound, communication
φῶς, φωτός, τό	light, torch

Χ χ

χαίρω	I am glad, rejoice, welcome
χαρά, ᾶς, ἡ	joy, delight, gladness
χάρις, ιτος, ἡ	grace, thankfulness, kindness
χείρ, χειρός, ἡ	hand
Χριστός, οῦ, ὁ	Messiah, Anointed One, Christ
χρόνος, ου, ὁ	time, occasion,

Ψ ψ

ψυχή, ῆς, ἡ	soul, life

Ω ω

ὧδε	*here, thus, in this way, exceedingly so*
ὥρα, ας, ἡ	*hour, time, period, season*
ὡς	*as, like*
ὥστε	*so that, therefore, consequently*

APPENDIX IV
KOINĒ GREEK PARADIGM CHARTS

Athematic (μι) Stems: no connecting vowels

	Primary Tense				Secondary/Historical Tense			
	Active		Middle/Passive		Active		Middle/Passive	
	Singular	Plural	Singular	Plural	Singular	Plural	Singular	Plural
1st	μι	μεν	μαι	μεθα	ν	μεν	μην	μεθα
2nd	ς	τε	σαι	σθε	ς	τε	σο	σθε
3rd	σι(ν)	ασι(ν)	ται	νται	-	σαν	το	ντο

Thematic (ω) Stems: connecting vowel included

	Primary Tense				Secondary/Historical Tense			
	Active		Middle/Passive		Active		Middle/Passive	
	Singular	Plural	Singular	Plural	Singular	Plural	Singular	Plural
1st	ω	ομεν	ομαι	ομεθα	ον	ομεν	ομην	ομεθα
2nd	εις	ετε	ῃ	εσθε	ες	ετε	ου	εσθε
3rd	ει	ουσι	εται	ονται	- / ε	ον	ετο	οντο

Imperative (using λύω)

			Active	Middle	Passive
Present	Singular	2nd	λῦε	λύου	
		3rd	λυέτω	λυέσθω	
	Plural	2nd	λύετε	λύεσθε	
		3rd	λυέτωσαν	λυέσθωσαν	
Aorist	Singular	2nd	λῦσον	λῦσαι	λύθητι
		3rd	λυσάτω	λυσάσθω	λυθήτω
	Plural	2nd	λύσατε	λύσασθε	λύθητε
		3rd	λυσάτωσαν	λυσάσθωσαν	λυθήτωσαν

Infinitive (using λύω)

	Active	Middle	Passive
Present	λυείν	λύεσθαι	
Aorist	λῦσαι	λύσασθαι	λυθῆναι
Perfect	λελυκέναι	λελύσθαι	

APPENDICES
Participle (using λύω)

			Present		Aorist			Perfect	
			Act.	Mid./Pass.	Act.	Mid.	Pass.	Act.	Mid./Pass.
Masculine	Singular	Nom.	λύων	λυόμενος	λύσας	λυσάμενος	λυθείς	λελυκώς	λελυμένος
		Gen.	λύοντος	λυομένου	λύσαντος	λυσαμένου	λυθέντος	λελυκότος	λελυμένου
		Dat.	λύοντι	λυομένῳ	λύσαντι	λυσαμένῳ	λυθέντι	λελυκότι	λελυμένῳ
		Acc.	λύοντα	λυόμενον	λύσαντα	λυσάμενον	λυθέντα	λελυκότα	λελυμένον
	Plural	Nom.	λύοντες	λυόμενοι	λύσαντες	λυσάμενοι	λυθέντες	λελυκότες	λελυμένοι
		Gen.	λυόντων	λυομένων	λυσάντων	λυσαμένων	λυθέντων	λελυκότων	λελυμένων
		Dat.	λύουσι(ν)	λυομένοις	λύσασι(ν)	λυσαμένοις	λυθεῖσι(ν)	λελυκόσι(ν)	λελυμένοις
		Acc.	λύοντας	λυομένους	λύσαντας	λυσαμένους	λυθέντας	λελυκότας	λελυμένους
Feminine	Singular	Nom.	λύουσα	λυομένη	λύσασα	λυσαμένη	λυθεῖσα	λελυκυῖα	λελυμένη
		Gen.	λυούσης	λυομένης	λυσάσης	λυσαμένης	λυθείσης	λελυκυίας	λελυμένης
		Dat.	λυούσῃ	λυομένῃ	λυσάσῃ	λυσαμένῃ	λυθείσῃ	λελυκυίᾳ	λελυμένῃ
		Acc.	λύουσαν	λυομένην	λύσασαν	λυσαμένην	λυθεῖσαν	λελυκυῖαν	λελυμένην
	Plural	Nom.	λύουσαι	λυόμεναι	λύσασαι	λυσάμεναι	λυθεῖσαι	λελυκυῖαι	λελυμέναι
		Gen.	λυουσῶν	λυομένων	λυσασῶν	λυσαμένων	λυθεισῶν	λελυκυιῶν	λελυμένων
		Dat.	λυούσαις	λυομέναις	λυσάσαις	λυσαμέναις	λυθείσαις	λελυκυίαις	λελυμέναις
		Acc.	λυούσας	λυομένας	λυσάσας	λυσαμένας	λυθείσας	λελυκυίας	λελυμένας
Neuter	Singular	Nom.	λῦον	λυόμενον	λῦσαν	λυσάμενον	λυθέν	λελυκός	λελυμένον
		Gen.	λύοντος	λυομένου	λύσαντος	λυσαμένου	λυθέντος	λελυκότος	λελυμένου
		Dat.	λύοντι	λυομένῳ	λύσαντι	λυσαμένῳ	λυθέντι	λελυκότι	λελυμένῳ
		Acc.	λῦον	λυόμενον	λῦσαν	λυσάμενον	λυθέν	λελυκός	λελυμένον
	Plural	Nom.	λύοντα	λυόμενα	λύσαντα	λυσάμενα	λυθέντα	λελυκότα	λελυμένα
		Gen.	λυόντων	λυομένων	λυσάντων	λυσαμένων	λυθέντων	λελυκότων	λελυμένων
		Dat.	λύουσι(ν)	λυομένοις	λύσασι(ν)	λυσαμένοις	λυθεῖσι(ν)	λελυκόσι(ν)	λελυμένοις
		Acc.	λύοντα	λυόμενα	λύσαντα	λυσάμενα	λυθέντα	λελυκότα	λελυμένα

Subjunctive
(Aor Act. add -σ-; Aor Pass. add -θ-)

	Active		Middle/Passive	
	Sing.	Plur.	Sing.	Plur.
1st	ω	ωμεν	ωμαι	ωμεθα
2nd	ῃς	ητε	ῃ	ησθε
3rd	ῃ	ωσι(ν)	ηται	ωνται

Optative

	Active		Middle/Passive	
	Sing.	Plur.	Sing.	Plur.
1st	μι / ν	μεν	μην	μεθα
2nd	ς	τε	σο	σθε
3rd	-	εν / σαν	το	ντο

Thematic Formation:
Pres: -οι + ending
Aor A/M: -σαιη + ending
Aor P: -θειη + ending

Athematic Formation:
Pres: -ιη or -ι + ending
Aor A/M/P: -ιη or -ι + ending

APPENDIX IV: KOINĒ GREEK PARADIGM CHARTS

Present Indicative

	Sing.	Plur.
1st	εἰμί	ἐσμέν
2nd	εἶ	ἐστέ
3rd	ἐστί(ν)	εἰσί(ν)

Imperfect Indicative

	Sing.	Plur.
1st	ἤμην	ἦμεν
2nd	ἦς	ἦτε
3rd	ἦν	ἦσαν

Future Indicative

	Sing.	Plur.
1st	ἔσομαι	ἐσόμεθα
2nd	ἔσῃ	ἔσεσθε
3rd	ἔσται	ἔσονται

Present Subjunctive

	Sing.	Plur.
1st	ὦ	ὦμεν
2nd	ᾖς	ἦτε
3rd	ᾖ	ὦσι(ν)

Present Imperative

	Sing.	Plur.
2nd	ἴσθι	ἔστε
3rd	ἔστω	ἔστωσαν

Present Optative

	Sing.	Plur.
1st	εἴην	εἶμεν/εἴημεν
2nd	εἴης	εἶτε/εἴητε
3rd	εἴη	εἶεν/εἴησαν

Infinitive

Present	εἶναι
Future	ἔσεσθαι

Present Participle

		Masc.	Fem.	Neut.
Singular	Nom.	ὤν	οὖσα	ὄν
	Gen.	ὄντος	οὔσης	ὄντος
	Dat.	ὄντι	οὔσῃ	ὄντι
	Acc.	ὄντα	οὖσαν	ὄν
Plural	Nom.	ὄντες	οὖσαι	ὄντα
	Gen.	ὄντων	οὐσῶν	ὄντων
	Dat.	οὖσι(ν)	οὔσαις	οὖσι(ν)
	Acc.	ὄντας	οὔσας	ὄντα

Definite Article

	Singular			Plural		
	Masc.	Fem.	Neut.	Masc.	Fem.	Neut.
Nom.	ὁ	ἡ	τό	οἱ	αἱ	τά
Gen.	τοῦ	τῆς	τοῦ	τῶν		
Dat.	τῷ	τῇ	τῷ	τοῖς	ταῖς	τοῖς
Acc.	τόν	τήν	τό	τούς	τάς	τά

APPENDICES
1st Declension Endings

	Singular				Plur.
	ε, ι, ρ	σ, ζ, ξ, ψ	all other	Masc.	
Nom.	α	α	η	ης	αι
Gen.	ας	ης	ης	ου	ων
Dat.	ᾳ	ῃ	ῃ	ῃ	αις
Acc.	αν	αν	ην	ην	ας

2nd Declension Endings

	Singular			Plural		
	Masc.	Fem.	Neut.	Masc.	Fem.	Neut.
Nom.	ος		ον	οι		α
Gen.	ου			ων		
Dat.	ῳ			οις		
Acc.	ον			ους		α

3rd Declension Endings

	Singular			Plural		
	Masc.	Fem.	Neut.	Masc.	Fem.	Neut.
Nom.	ς / -		-	ες		α
Gen.	ος			ων		
Dat.	ι			σι(ν)		
Acc.	α / ν		-	ας / ες		α

πᾶς, πᾶσα, πᾶν | 3-1-3

	Singular			Plural		
	Masc.	Fem.	Neut.	Masc.	Fem.	Neut.
Nom.	πᾶς	πᾶσα	πᾶν	πάντες	πᾶσαι	πάντα
Gen.	παντός	πάσης	παντός	πάντων	πασῶν	πάντων
Dat.	παντί	πάσῃ	παντί	πᾶσι(ν)	πάσαις	πᾶσι(ν)
Acc.	πάντα	πᾶσαν	πᾶν	πάντας	πάσας	πάντα

πολύς, πολλή, πολύ | 2-1-2

	Singular			Plural		
	Masc.	Fem.	Neut.	Masc.	Fem.	Neut.
Nom.	πολύς	πολλή	πολύ	πολλοί	πολλαί	πολλά
Gen.	πολλοῦ	πολλῆς	πολλοῦ	πολλῶν		
Dat.	πολλῷ	πολλῇ	πολλῷ	πολλοῖς	πολλαῖς	πολλοῖς
Acc.	πολύν	πολλήν	πολύ	πολλούς	πολλάς	πολλά

APPENDIX IV: KOINĒ GREEK PARADIGM CHARTS

Personal Pronouns: *I, we, you, she, he, it, they*

	1st		2nd					3rd		
							Singular		Plural	
	Sing.	Plur.	Sing.	Plur.		Masc.	Fem.	Neut.	Masc.	Fem.	Neut.
Nom.	ἐγώ	ἡμεῖς	σύ	ὑμεῖς	Nom.	αὐτός	αὐτή	αὐτό	αὐτοί	αὐταί	αὐτά
Gen.	(ἐ)μοῦ	ἡμῶν	σοῦ	ὑμῶν	Gen.	αὐτοῦ	αὐτῆς	αὐτοῦ	αὐτῶν		
Dat.	(ἐ)μοί	ἡμῖν	σοί	ὑμῖν	Dat.	αὐτῷ	αὐτῇ	αὐτῷ	αὐτοῖς	αὐταῖς	αὐτοῖς
Acc.	(ἐ)μέ	ἡμᾶς	σέ	ὑμᾶς	Acc.	αὐτόν	αὐτήν	αὐτό	αὐτούς	αὐτάς	αὐτά

Proximal (Near) Demonstrative: *this, these*

	Singular			Plural		
	Masc.	Fem.	Neut.	Masc.	Fem.	Neut.
Nom.	οὗτος	αὕτη	τοῦτο	οὗτοι	αὗται	ταῦτα
Gen.	τούτου	ταύτης	τούτου	τούτων		
Dat.	τούτῳ	ταύτῃ	τούτῳ	τούτοις	ταύταις	τούτοις
Acc.	τοῦτον	ταύτην	τοῦτο	τούτους	ταύτας	ταῦτα

Distal (Far) Demonstrative: *that, those*

	Singular			Plural		
	Masc.	Fem.	Neut.	Masc.	Fem.	Neut.
Nom.	ἐκεῖνος	ἐκείνη	ἐκεῖνο	ἐκεῖνοι	ἐκεῖναι	ἐκεῖνα
Gen.	ἐκείνου	ἐκείνης	ἐκείνου	ἐκείνων		
Dat.	ἐκείνῳ	ἐκείνῃ	ἐκείνῳ	ἐκείνοις	ἐκείναις	ἐκείνοις
Acc.	ἐκεῖνον	ἐκείνην	ἐκεῖνο	ἐκείνους	ἐκείνας	ἐκεῖνα

Interrogative Pronouns: *who? which? what?*

	Singular		Plural	
	Masc. Fem.	Neut.	Masc. Fem.	Neut.
Nom.	τίς	τί	τίνες	τίνα
Gen.	τίνος		τίνων	
Dat.	τίνι		τίσι(ν)	
Acc.	τίνα	τί	τίνας	τίνα

Indefinite Pronouns: *someone, something*

	Singular		Plural	
	Masc. Fem.	Neut.	Masc. Fem.	Neut.
Nom.	τις	τι	τινες	τινα
Gen.	τινος		τινων	
Dat.	τινι		τισι(ν)	
Acc.	τινα	τι	τινας	τινα

APPENDICES

Indefinite Relative Pronouns: *whoever, whichever, every one who*

	Singular			Plural		
	Masc.	Fem.	Neut.	Masc.	Fem.	Neut.
Nom.	ὅστις	ἥτις	ὅ τι / ὅτι	οἵτινες	αἵτινες	ἅτινα
Gen.	οὕτινος	ἧστινος	οὕτινος	ὥντινων		
Dat.	ᾧτινι	ᾗτινι	ᾧτινι	οἷστισι(ν)	αἷστισι(ν)	οἷστισι(ν)
Acc.	ὅντινα	ἥντινα	ὅ τι / ὅτι	οὕστινας	ἅστινας	ἅτινα

Reciprocal Pronouns: *one another*

	Plural
Gen.	ἀλλήλων
Dat.	ἀλλήλοις
Acc.	ἀλλήλους

Relative Pronouns: *who, which, that*

	Singular			Plural		
	M	F	N	M	F	N
Nom.	ὅς	ἥ	ὅ	οἵ	αἵ	ἅ
Gen.	οὗ	ἧς	οὗ	ὧν		
Dat.	ᾧ	ᾗ	ᾧ	οἷς	αἷς	οἷς
Acc.	ὅν	ἥν	ὅ	οὕς	ἅς	ἅ

Reflexive Pronouns: *myself, yourself, herself, himself, itself*

		1st		2nd		3rd		
		Masc.	Fem.	Masc.	Fem.	Masc.	Fem.	Neut.
Singular	Gen.	ἐμαυτοῦ	ἐμαυτῆς	σεαυτοῦ	σεαυτῆς	ἑαυτοῦ	ἑαυτῆς	ἑαυτοῦ
	Dat.	ἐμαυτῷ	ἐμαυτῇ	σεαυτῷ	σεαυτῇ	ἑαυτῷ	ἑαυτῇ	ἑαυτῷ
	Acc.	ἐμαυτόν	ἐμαυτήν	σεαυτόν	σεαυτήν	ἑαυτόν	ἑαυτήν	ἑαυτό
Plural	Gen.	ἑαυτῶν		ἑαυτῶν		ἑαυτῶν		
	Dat.	ἑαυτοῖς	ἑαυταῖς	ἑαυτοῖς	ἑαυταῖς	ἑαυτοῖς	ἑαυταῖς	ἑαυτοῖς
	Acc.	ἑαυτούς	ἑαυτάς	ἑαυτούς	ἑαυτάς	ἑαυτούς	ἑαυτάς	ἑαυτά

www.ingramcontent.com/pod-product-compliance
Lightning Source LLC
Chambersburg PA
CBHW071739080526
44588CB00013B/2094